THE BOOK OF AGREEMENT AND REMEMBRANCE

THE BOOK OF
AGREEMENT
AND
REMEMBRANCE

Developing a Healthy
Christian Marriage

CHRIS BROUGHTON

THE BOOK OF AGREEMENT AND REMEMBRANCE
DEVELOPING A HEALTHY CHRISTIAN MARRIAGE

Author Credits: Genesis 2:24 Ministries

Unless otherwise indicated, all scripture quotations are taken from THE HOLY BIBLE, NEW INTERNATIONAL VERSION®, NIV® Copyright © 1973, 1978, 1984, 2011 by Biblica, Inc.® Used by permission. All rights reserved worldwide.

iUniverse books may be ordered through booksellers or by contacting:

iUniverse
1663 Liberty Drive
Bloomington, IN 47403
www.iuniverse.com
1-800-Authors (1-800-288-4677)

Because of the dynamic nature of the Internet, any web addresses or links contained in this book may have changed since publication and may no longer be valid. The views expressed in this work are solely those of the author and do not necessarily reflect the views of the publisher, and the publisher hereby disclaims any responsibility for them.

Any people depicted in stock imagery provided by Getty Images are models, and such images are being used for illustrative purposes only. Certain stock imagery © Getty Images.

ISBN: 978-1-5320-6389-3 (sc)
ISBN: 978-1-5320-6394-7 (hc)
ISBN: 978-1-5320-6390-9 (e)

Print information available on the last page.

iUniverse rev. date: 02/14/2019

Contents

Foreword

It had to be somewhere around 1997 when I first met Chris and his lovely wife Gay. That's right we go back to the 1900s, you can say we have been friends along time. One thing I cherish about our friendship is that Chris is not just my friend, he is a friend of my family and a friend of my friends. We do life together as we are gifted the time and opportunities.

You will come across a story of a neighbor child and her perception of Chris and Gay. She never separates the two from each other. That is what inspires me most about the man who has written this book. He does life the way God instructed it to be done, "the two shall be one."

In your hands you may recognize a book. Perhaps it is a modern-day epistle on marriage. It is written as inspired of the Holy Spirit. Presented as one who has an authority. Any and all concepts from the Book of Agreement are scripturally found and personally experienced. And I have witnessed the fruit of such a life lived by two who have become one!

Your time reading will not be wasted. Enjoy it and explore it! Just as the epistles of the greatest book ever written remain relevant and evident. So, you will find this book to be a manual for you to experience a blessed and prosperous marriage.

In Him,
Greg DeVries
Lead Pastor, The Well

Introduction

About Genesis 2:24 Ministries

For years my wife Gay and I watched our friends and fellow Christians suffer from the pain of divorce. This broke our hearts. In 1999 we decided to do something about it and established Genesis 2:24 ministries as an outreach to help couples learn to live together happily. We worked mostly in southern Indiana with individual couples but also held group studies. In 2008 Genesis 2:24 Ministries was organized as a not-for-profit corporation in the state of Indiana. The ministry has a 501c3 designation as a religious organization. Chris and Gay Broughton are a pastoral couple associated with the EMIF organization in Scottsboro, Alabama.

The mission of Genesis 2:24 Ministries: "To Restore Marriage to the place of honor described in God's Word".

The Vision of Genesis 2:24 Ministries is to see divorce abolished in our lifetime.

We want to see God's plan for marriage realized in every marital relationship. Genesis 2:24 Ministries does individual couples coaching, group teaching and ministry support. Our services are always free and with the advent of technology, we have found we can reach nearly anyone by using services such as facetime and skype.

About this book

Thank you for the opportunity to help you and your spouse to live happily ever after. I count it as a privilege and pray that God will bless you through the words I have written here.

Why did I write a book about agreement and remembrance?

Since we founded Genesis 2:24 Ministries in 1999, we have seen a wide variety of marital problems. The problems come in a myriad of sizes, shapes, and colors but have one recurring theme: disagreement and disunity. We believe a marriage built on common agreement with God and his plan for marriage will provide a couple with all they need to live happily ever after in peace and unity.

We have spent more than half of our married life coaching couples to live happily ever after and through those experiences we have developed a number of tools and tactics. Couples with who we are working often remark, "It sure would help if you would write these lessons down so we can get help when you are not around." The "Book of Agreement and Remembrance" is one of the tools we teach. This book is the lessons and tactics needed to implement your own "Book of Agreement and Remembrance" … written down.

The contents of this book are principles and tactics my wife, Gay, and I have been teaching to couples for more than 20 years. They are well-tested we know that you will benefit from these writings as you learn to agree and live in unity. It is our prayer that your marriage profits from these lessons as you learn to travel through your married life together and in agreement.

Who is this book written for?

The short answer is you, or at least I hope so. I believe it is God's desire that all will have life and have it abundantly. I believe we were created to be married <u>and</u> to be married happily. I believe God's plan is to have us enjoy agreement, unity, and intimacy in our marriage. The purpose of this book is to teach agreement and unity with one another through lessons and tactics we have developed and adapted from the Bible.

If you are not yet a believer, the principles and tactics taught here may be hard for you to understand and perhaps even harder to adopt and use. Please understand, I am not saying the tactics in this book will not work for those not yet born again. I am saying, it will be difficult for you to understand why these principles work and you may have difficulty with their application to your life. Sometimes that difficulty will add to an already frustrating situation. Please hold your frustration at arm's length and consider allowing Holy Spirit to show you his wisdom as you read the scripture presented here.

It is my strong desire for every married couple to live happily ever together. I also know that 100% of the time when individuals are following Christ they do not have problems within their marriage relationship. So, if you have found yourself here and have not yet given your life to Christ, please reach out to me at www.genesis2-24.net and I will connect you with someone that can introduce you to Jesus. You will be glad you did.

Meet Charlie and Harriet

Some friends had invited us to the dedication of their first son. They had also invited Charlie and Harriet whom they had known since high school. Charlie and Harriet were to be named the Godparents during the celebration.

We sat next to Charlie and Harriet at the picnic celebration after church. They knew a little about our ministry and the book I published in 2012 titled "21 Days to Happily Ever After."

Once we were all seated Charlie asks me "I hear you have cracked the code to have a happy marriage."

"I like to think so" I chuckled "I'm pretty happy."

"Well then, explain this one to me. I have to hold out a little money for myself or Harriet spends it all." He said as he stabbed his thumb in the air toward his wife. "I have a little hidey-hole I keep it in where she can't get at it."

Turns out Harriet had recently discovered his little "hidey-hole" and was livid about it. Charlie claimed she had made a "Federal Case" about it and needed to just "Chill Out!."

"After all, I work hard, I should be able to keep a little mad money that is mine, shouldn't I"?

Charlie was looking for ruling from me on the matter. His wife had been listening as well to see if the men would gang up on her.

"I am not so sure about that," I started. "Do you guys have a budget?"

"Yeah sure, I pay my bills she pays hers, and then we use the rest the way we please, we do alright." The volume with which he answered suggested offense and that perhaps I had stuck my nose a little too deep in his business.

Charlie was offended because he thought I was telling him to tighten his belt and spend less. He jumped to the conclusion that their fight was about the amount of money they had. What I really wanted to know was if he and his wife had agreed on how to spend the money they did have.

So, I followed up with, "Do you know what it costs to run your household every month?"

He raised his voice a little more, sat a little closer to the edge of his seat, leaned in and said, "Like I said, we do OK, I pay my bills."

"I understand, but I am trying to find out if you agree about money. And I am 100% sure you have not agreed if you do not know the facts, and I am thinking this is a sore subject between the two of you. It's not about the amount of money you do or do not have or who spends what, your problem is your lack of agreement about money."

Harriet and Charlie are like so many couples we encounter. They have not learned to put away selfishness and to agree with one another before situations arise. Make no mistake life will constantly present new situations that demand your attention. If you already have a plan to handle it, and you have a way to bring that plan to remembrance, life is easy. Lack of a plan and a way to bring it to remembrance will lead to dis-unity in any relationship, but this lack will become unbearable in a marriage relationship.

Will reading this book fix all my marriage problems?

Nope. It is unlikely that your marriage will become suddenly better because you purchased this book (or any book for that matter). There is no quick fix. You will need to decide to apply what you learn from the lessons presented here, then allow God to bring the difference.

I once bought a book that promised to have the answer to my blood pressure problem. It was a good read, but it ended with directions on dietary changes I needed to make to actually see a drop in my blood pressure. Giving up pickles and olives was more than I was willing to do at the time, so the book did me no good.

The better question is "Will my marriage prosper from living in unity through agreement with my spouse?" The answer to that question is a resounding YES. Unity, or what we often call "becoming one-flesh", is God's plan for every married couple. This book will present a definition of Biblical unity in marriage, a false view of what the world sees as agreement and finally a tried-and-true method to break free of the false view and live in truth.

If you have the discipline to apply these principles, it is my belief that God will bless you in ways you have never seen or thought possible. You will have peace in your home as promised by Jesus (the Prince of Peace) and will enjoy living in a place I like to call "Happily Ever After."

Why read this book and practice the principles in it?

Unfortunately, disagreement in a married relationship is common. It is something our culture sees as normal. But disagreement provides a toehold for the enemy and disharmony ruins true intimacy and happiness in married relationships. When a couple learns how to walk in agreement, they can spend their energy and passion for more important matters, like being in love with one another.

Who are the couples mentioned in this book?

Gay and I founded Genesis 2:24 Ministries to help couples know God's plan for marriage and to help them walk a path that leads to the bliss and blessings intended for them as one-flesh. Over the years we have had the privilege to work with hundreds of couples. We have also determined that Satan is the enemy of marriage and works to destroy all marriages, but he is not very creative. So, we see some common themes played out time and again. To help illustrate the principles presented in this book, I have created fictional couples to represent a composite view of those themes. Any resemblance to anyone specific is purely accidental. I hope that you will see yourself in these fictitious couples and their troubles, conversations, and actions. I also hope their troubles and victories will help you recognize the tactics of your enemy, Satan.

Eric and Megan

When I first met Eric and his wife Megan, she was on his last nerve. I was a guest at a friend's house during a Bluegrass Jam. He was a banjo player who liked to drink. The host of the Jam brought Eric over to me, pointed his finger uncomfortably close to my nose and said something like, "this is the guy that thinks he has marriage all figured out." My friend slaps me on the back, throws his head back, laughs again and walks off. Bewildered and not knowing what to do with that introduction, I just kept playing music and smiled at Eric.

During a break, Eric sought me out and told me that he and his wife spent too much time fighting. He wanted to know the secret to getting her to stop nagging. "WOW, that is a tall order," I told him. "What's all the nagging about?"

"Well this jam for example, first she doesn't want to come, then she does. When we get here she tells me not to drink too much. Then 3 hours later, she catches a ride home and leaves me here." He then gives me the universal hand signal for a question mark, followed by hands in the "hands up I'm innocent" manner and shrugs his shoulders. All this action caused him to spill a little beer from his red solo cup.

"So, do you want her to come with you"?

"Yeah, I love her and miss her when she isn't here, but I need a little peace."

Turns out he wanted peace in his home as well. He and Megan fought about more than Bluegrass Jams and how much beer he drank while playing. They would fight at home about bedtime or discipline for the kids and how often his mother should come over. They would fight at the grocery store about whole milk versus two percent. They once fought, in public, over the color of the car they were buying so badly that Eric had to walk home after Megan left in an Uber with the car keys in her pocket. It seemed that they disagreed about almost everything.

Eric then told me that his lawyer had told him it sounded like they had "Irreconcilable differences" and that a divorce may be his only course of action to have peace. That raised my emotions to a point where I was vacillating between smacking Eric or burning down his lawyer's office. But before I sinned in my anger, I asked Eric, "What is it that you want"?

"I want to live in harmony and peace with my wife and kids in my home," he said. "Look I am a Christian, and I take my wedding vows seriously, but I just can't keep living on the edge of this constant storm."

Like most married couples they don't fight about every little thing for the joy of the fight. I knew that they simply did not have the tools to agree and to remember their agreements. This may sound like double-talk on the surface: it did to Eric and Megan as well. But over the next six months as we walked them through the lessons taught in this book they saw peace rise in their home. In the same way, the tide of ocean raises all the ships, so their new peace made everyone happy. It is my prayer you will see the same overwhelming peace come over your life as well.

Where do I start?

I think you have started already. You are reading this book, so you are thinking about living in agreement with your spouse: keep reading. While you read and study, be sure to have a couple of other important tools handy:

1) Your Personal Bible. Scripture is quoted throughout this book and I encourage you to look them up in your own Bible so that you read them in the translation you like best. You may also want to make notes in your Bible if Holy Spirit reveals something new to you. Yes, friends, it is OK to write in the margins, underline, highlight or even draw pictures if it helps to personalize the Word for you. I personally find it helpful to also date those notes, highlights, underlines, and pictures.

2) Have a journal and write down what God reveals to you as you grow. God has promised his word will not return void but will accomplish its purpose – which is to grow and prosper you. Your journal will also provide a place to witness (remembrance) of God's glory in your life. Your personal journal can be anything that you will keep handy - I personally use very inexpensive theme books I find on sale at my local office supply store. **The point is, I want you to journal.**

3) If you have questions or comments about this book, our ministry or us, please do not hesitate to contact us at www.genesis2-24.net.

The beginning: God's plan for marriage

Coming together is a beginning; keeping together is progress; working together is success. (Henry Ford)

This section of the book is meant to provide a place to start to lay a foundation. From there we build the house. Jesus said that if we want our house to stand when the rain and floods come we will need to build it on solid rock. (Matthew 7:24)

Last summer I needed to replace a small piece of trim on the outside of my house. My tallest stepladder was too short to reach it. My best friend has an extension ladder that would have worked, but I was in a hurry to check this off my to-do list. I backed my pick-up truck near enough the front porch to put two legs on the porch and two on the tailgate of my truck. What I had not accounted for was the rear shocks interaction with my weight on the tailgate. I climbed in the bed of the truck and up the ladder. The ladder shifted, I wobbled and visions of broken things (legs and arms) danced in my head. I climbed down rather quickly, with a better understanding of the dangers of a shaky foundation. My haste to complete the task was about to become a matter of record at the emergency room.

I want you to have a rock-solid foundation about God's plan for marriage. Something you can stand on and reach agreement, a foundation that will stand against the very gates of Hell. Take your time with these principles, make them a part of your life and your relationship. Don't hurry to check each chapter off as if you were finishing some to do list.

In beginning God created.

> Haven't you read," he replied, "that at the beginning the Creator 'made them male and female, and said, 'For this reason, a man will leave his father and mother and be united to his wife, and the two will become one flesh? So, they are no longer two, but one flesh. Therefore what God has joined together, let no one separate. (Matthew 19:4-6)

God's call for agreement in marriage began, well, in the beginning. I mean the beginning of time… the "in the beginning" spoken of in Genesis. God's plan for marriage calls us to become "one flesh" when we marry and much of the remainder of the Bible is a roadmap of how to walk in agreement as one flesh. Ok, that was easy enough… right? No? Not really?

Let's take a closer look at God's plan for mankind which includes a definition of what agreement in marriage looks like.

Who invented marriage and why?

This is a subject we always talk about during individual marital counseling session. We usually start by asking "Who do you think invented marriage?" We get a lot of answers like "the government" or "the Bible" but the most common answer is "I don't know." The right answer is God. God invented marriage as a part of his perfect plan for his creation. In the first two chapters of the Bible, he made us male and female and created us to be husbands and wives.

Genesis Chapter 1 is a macro-view account of the creation of everything. The scriptures walk us through a day by day account of God creating the heavens, the earth, and all the plants and animals in days one through five. On day six "God created mankind in his own image, in the image of God he created them; male and female he created them" (Genesis 1:26).

In Chapter 2 we get a more detailed description of the creation of men and women and why they were created. Adam was created first and placed in the garden to cultivate and care for it. God gave him instructions about the garden and two trees in the middle of the garden. (Genesis 2:15-17). God recognized that it was not good for man to be alone (Genesis 2:18). So, the search for a "helper suitable" began (Genesis 2:19-20). Imagine how long it took for God to show Adam every animal created and then to have Adam name every one of them. If he called it a monkey, that was what it would be called. A dog is a dog because Adam called it a dog. Every animal from aardvark to zebra was presented to Adam and he named them. What is important here is that Adam never named any of the animals, "woman." He never looked at anything in all of creation and named it "helper suitable." So, God created something new and perfect to be his perfect helpmate.

God the Father created woman while Adam slept (Genesis 2:21). He then took his daughter by the hand, walked her down the aisle and presented her to Adam. Adam exclaimed, "Now this is bone of my bone and flesh of my flesh." In southern Indiana redneck that can be translated into "Now that's what I'm talkin' 'bout." She was what he had been asking God for, what he had been looking for and exactly what he needed. God the Father presented his daughter, Eve, to her husband and performed the first wedding. He pronounced that they would be one flesh and have perfect intimacy by being naked and unashamed (Genesis 2:24-25).

Consider this… It is not good for man to be alone (Genesis 2:18) and the woman was never meant to be alone (Genesis 2:18 & 22). We were created as individuals that need one another and are called to leave our current life and cling to one another as one flesh. That one flesh relationship is to be an intimate "naked and unashamed" relationship (Genesis 2:24-25). Let's talk about each of those ideas.

What does it mean to leave and cleave?

God intended for us to be raised by our parents and then to leave their house to start a new life with our spouse. A new and unique creation with a new and unique home in which to raise up our own family. This is not an act of disrespect or abandonment of family and ancestry but rather an act of multiplying. My surname is Broughton as was my father's and his father before him. My dad (George) married my mom (Carol) and they established a home very different and unique from their parents' homes. The family and home I established with Gay is very different from the home I grew up. As expected my son is different than me but we are all called "Broughton."

When I married Gay, we began to form our own traditions and celebrations. The first year we were married we went on a picnic on Christmas Day to try out the new backpacking camp stove Gay had given me. We sat next to a frozen creek and I prepared a wonderful meal and served it on my new aluminum mess kits. My mother was stunned and frankly a little disappointed that we did not come to her house and enjoy all my favorite foods from my childhood as I had for the previous 25 Christmases of my life.

This is all part of the leaving, but we need to cleave to one another as well…

Gay and I met and married while in college in 1979. Rock concerts were cheap and plentiful back then and were an essential part of what I did with my free time. My hippie friends and I would load up in the designated driver's car and see a show nearly every weekend. Gay enjoyed the same music but was not overly fond of the rowdy crowds. She was uncomfortable when mashed in a confined space with 10,000 sweaty, screaming rowdies in front of speakers so loud the air pressure would actually move your clothes and hair. I came to understand and appreciate that I preferred Gay's company over anything and anyone else (including the hearing loss from a great ZZ Top live show). Instead, Gay and I started listening to records on the stereo cranked to "11" in the comfort of our own home: Less hearing loss AND time spent with my perfect helper.

I left my old life with its traditions, habits and in some cases, people, and started to cling to my new life with Gay. For nearly 40 years now we have grown, changed, and developed many new interests and traditions. Because we both first left our old lives and learned to cling to one another, we grew together in true intimacy, as one flesh and naked and unashamed.

Simply put leaving our old life and cleaving to the new one is the only way to a level of intimacy that will allow you to become one flesh and to be truly naked and unashamed.

What is one flesh?

In the first five years of my marriage to Gay, we lived next door to a young family in Florida. Their young daughter, Sara, would wander over to our house, knock on the door and ask for "Chris and Gay." If she saw me in the yard she would shout out "Hi, Chris and Gay." If Gay was pushing her in the swing she would giggle and say, "Higher, Chris and Gay." She thought each of us had the same name and never thought to separate us into two different entities. I did not realize at the time what a great compliment she was paying us. I can only pray that the world still sees "Chris and Gay" and not me standing alone without my perfect helper.

Each of us is created as an individual that can be uniquely identified by our fingerprints, our history, our ancestry, our personality and our way of thinking. We are like no one else that exists today, no one who has ever been or ever will be. The fact that we are unique in history is evidence of the incredible, magnificent, and unimaginable creativity of God. Marriage is an extension of his plan of creation. God creates a new and unique one flesh creation with each marriage. There does not exist today, nor ever was there ever and never again will be there be another one flesh team like you and your spouse. You as a couple are unique in his eyes and in his heart. And you have been called to a unique place of unity and peace that no other one flesh team will ever achieve.

Genesis 2:24 describes how that new creation is to be created. We are to leave our old lives and all that is connected to it and to become one flesh with our spouse. Jesus repeated this to us in Matthew 19:5 to help us remember that the idea of divorce is a perversion of God's plan for marriage and is an act of tearing apart something God has put together.

The concept of two becoming one is in many ways difficult for us to understand and therefore difficult to adopt as a way of life. The best evidence of society's lack of understanding of one flesh is demonstrated by our celebrating the coming together at weddings and then 52% of those same marriages ending in divorce. Our culture teaches us to be individuals first and then continue "to thine own self be true." Oh, by the way, this is a quote from Shakespeare's Hamlet, not the Bible.

Becoming one flesh is rooted in the very nature of God's creative power. Often our modern way of thinking resists the creative power of God because it runs contrary to how we think the world works. Ideas like love your enemy, give away 10% of your income or forgive even when they don't deserve it are considered obsolete in the modern world. It is no wonder we have trouble understanding one flesh because so much of our culture is opposed to God's plan for the marriage founded on this principle. Here are some examples:

- We are taught to never lose our personal identity in marriage.
- We work very hard at maintaining cultural ties to who we were before marriage, often at the expense of who we are to become in marriage.
- We are taught to stand up for our personal rights ahead of our personal responsibilities.

We end up fighting with the very people with whom we have committed to do life with. This resistance to God's creative plan for our marriage will prevent agreement in our one flesh relationship and so hinders unity in marriage. If you will commit to follow God's creative plan for marriage and become one flesh, you can live in the peace and unity only available from God himself.

The beginning of unity in marriage is to create a new family with new traditions and new ways of doing things; a new life. A new life that is a permanent relationship so close that you can no longer see two only but one. A new life that is unique; like no other and rooted in the truth of God's Word. To become truly one flesh requires that each of you be naked and unashamed in a covenant relationship.

What is naked and unashamed?

> Adam and his wife were both naked, and they
> felt no shame. (Genesis 2:25)

Many of us have read this and heard it any number of times but I would suggest you read it with new ears right now. I come from Southern Indiana and there are two ways to pronounce the word "Naked." There is NAKED which means you don't have clothes on. Then there is "NECKED" which is you don't have clothes on and you're up to something. I am a strong proponent of both of these within the marriage relationship, but I want to concentrate on NAKED right now. I promise the NECKED is so much better when you are well practiced in the NAKED.

Being NAKED here means that your spouse can see all of you. But there is more to this naked than meets the eye, that is, it is more than your skin. It means your spouse is allowed to see all of you, your thoughts and desires, your likes and dislikes, what makes you happy and what makes you sad. When you slip and do something that you are not proud of, can your spouse know about it? Can you know the same about them? Adam and Eve were so close that they felt no shame. They could allow the other to see them completely, warts and all.

This scripture sounds so simple but is perhaps one of the hardest scriptures in the Bible to put into practice within a marriage. It is rare for a man and his wife to be truly naked AND feel no shame. This is a source of many misunderstandings because it is the basis of misinformation.

During a pre-marital counseling session, we heard a bride talk about being on the LGN diet in preparation for her wedding. I thought I had heard of and tried most fad diets, but this was a new one, so I asked for more information. She then clarified that she was on the "LOOK GOOD NAKED" diet so that the first time her new husband saw her without clothes he would be pleased. This crash diet would for sure help her physical appearance for a time but was not centered on being honest with her future husband. I wondered, would she feel shame when she gained the 20lbs back shortly after the wedding? Would she begin to hide from her husband? Did he secretly want her thinner than she was at present? What else could they be hiding from one another?

Meet Mark and Libby

The first step to getting individual coaching from us is to fill out a form that helps us know where to start. One of the questions is "Tell us about what brought you to us" and then we leave a few lines for them to answer. Ninety percent of the forms we receive list communication as the problem.

Mark and Libby were one of those couples. They listed "constant fighting and lack of communication" as the most important area in which they wanted our help. It was our second meeting with them and we wanted to begin work on this priority. One thing we have learned over the last 20 years of meeting with couples is that arguments are rarely really about what you are yelling at one another, but are rooted in a deeper problem with a lack of intimacy (In-to-me-see).

Gay asked "You mentioned that you fight all the time and need help learning to communicate. What sorts of things do you disagree about?"

Libby jumped in quickly and described how she wished Mark would just stop yelling at her and the kids all the time. She ended with a reenactment of Mark on a rampage over some trivial matter around the house.

Mark retorted with "Yeah but, you are the one that is constantly screaming at me and the kids about how hard you work around the house and we don't appreciate it. You always seem to find something I didn't do right and want me to fix it, but you don't want to tell me what is wrong with it."

"Well, if you can't figure it out by now, I don't know why I keep trying," Libby said as she moved to the edge of her seat.

The faces were getting red and the voices were raising so I waved my hands in the air and said, "Whoa, time out."

"So, it seems that you both would agree that it could be quieter and more peaceful around your house," Gay asked. They both nodded rather vigorously. "Anything else?"

The next twenty minutes was a roller coaster ride of raised emotion followed by my calling for calm and Gay probing more into what goes on around Mark and Libby's house. At the end of the exercise, we had a list of the things that they wanted to change. The list counted any number of offenses each of them had committed against the other and a category we decided to call "things that really make me mad."

It was easy to see there was little unity in this house. So, we started where all good answers come from, the Bible. We read Genesis Chapter 3:1-7 together. Which ends with

> Then the eyes of both of them were opened, and they realized they were **naked**; so they sewed fig leaves together and made coverings for themselves (Genesis 3:7)

We needed to work with Mark and Libby to get them to remove the fig leaves they had sewn together to hide from one another. They were constantly talking about how each other's actions were wrong but not willing to tell one another how the action made them feel. For example:

Libby could not stand the way Mark kept the top of his dresser. It seemed that he was piling stuff on the top of stuff and it made her nervous. She would never talk to him about that because she thought it was too personal. She would however, complain that Mark did not help her keep the house clean hoping he would take the hint. She was never honest with him about what was bothering her, and he never probed deep to understand what she was really asking him to do.

The practice of covering up what you are thinking or what you need will hinder your ability to remain in the marriage relationship as God intended – in a covenant relationship

What is a covenant relationship?

So often we hear couples in distress tell us that "Well, I am doing my best, but it takes two to make this work." I am not sure that is as true as we have been led to believe. If we are truly in a marriage covenant and not a marriage contract it only takes one to get the ball rolling. Let me explain the difference.

A contract is completely performance based. If I do my part, then the other party is compelled to do their part. If the other party fails to fulfill any part of the contract, I am relieved from doing any of my parts. This is like when I buy a car on credit. As long as I make the payments they let me keep the car. If I stop making payments, they come to get the car.

Mark and Libby were constantly bargaining with one another as a tactic to solve problems. Mark would skip the driving range on Thursday if he could have "Saturday off" to go play a round of golf and Libby would be allowed to stay in town late and go to dinner with some of her girlfriends one night a week. One particular week Libby had forgotten about a birthday party that required the whole family to attend, on a Saturday. Mark was upset because he had done his part of the "bargain" but had not received his payment. The fight Saturday morning centered around how he had the <u>right</u> to be compensated for his effort or perhaps he would just call off the deal altogether and make Libby pick up the kids every day from now on.

A covenant relationship requires each partner to trade any and all individual rights for responsibility to and for the other. There can be no limits put on the liability of the partners. Limits on the liability or a claim of rights create a performance-based or "contractual" relationship. In a covenant relationship, each partner is completely responsible for and accountable to the other partner. I will do my part, no matter what the other party does. Period, full stop, no ifs, ands or buts about it… I will do my part.

We always ask couples with whom we do counseling "What are the show stoppers, the deal breakers, what will make you file for divorce?" What we are really asking is are you in a contract or a covenant relationship? More times than not there are conditions on them staying in the marriage. The conditions can be anything from the man develops a beer gut to the woman cheats on him. The truth is that there are no conditions in God's plan for marriage, only a plan to miraculously become one flesh and never to allow for divorce.

Marriage is meant to be a covenant, but the world likes to treat it like a contract. For example, a man agrees to mow the lawn on Saturday but goes fishing instead and his wife withholds sex from him as a result. He did not do his part so she does not have to do hers. Or the wife spends money on an expensive dress for a party they are planning to attend so the husband is justified to purchase fishing tackle of an equal amount. These examples are neither healthy for the relationship nor biblical.

Take a moment to check your vitals

Before you move on to the next chapter, take a moment and read the scriptures. If you can, read them with your spouse. Let them be a lamp unto your feet and a light with which to see your marriage. Ask yourself, "Am I in a covenant?" "Can I be naked and unashamed?" Ask God what he thinks. This is not an opportunity to beat yourself or your spouse up but rather a time of looking into yourself so that you can allow your spouse to "IN-TO-ME-SEE".

Common problems in marriage

Marriage is often studied. The Center for Disease Control's National Vital Statistics website suggests that marriages have been ending in divorce at a rate of about 50% for the last 16 years. [1] We learn from the US Census that fewer adults are choosing to be married nowadays.[2] There are talk shows and reality shows competing to tell us the most shocking situations couples put themselves and their marriages into and how to resolve them.

Gay and I have been a little less formal in our study of marriage but after years of hearing couples tell us what they think is wrong, we have developed a short list. The list of things that will either kill or vitalize a marriage is not really all that long and not really all that complicated. As I mentioned in other places in this book, Satan is your enemy and he only has a few tricks. He is not very creative and so he uses the same old tricks over and over. Here is my short list of tricks of the enemy.

---

[1] Source: CDC/NCHS National Vital Statistics System (Published 2017)

[2] Source: U.S. Census Bureau, Current Population Survey, March and Annual Social and Economic Supplements. (Published 2017)

Sex and Money

These are the top two reasons people mention when they tell us they are having problems. Ninety-seven percent of the time sex and money are listed as problems that caused a couple to divorce. Sometimes couples will try to disguise these by calling it a communication problem or perhaps claim their spouse is not there for them. Or the husband will tell us that his wife does not say she loves him enough or talk with him. What he is really saying he is wanting more sex and she won't give it to him.

Both of these are things for which we feel passion. Both are areas of deep perversion in our society and can be things that we sometimes lust after. How do I know this? First, because the Bible teaches it. Second, because I have walked through both problems in my life and in my marriage.

The longest fight ever

Once in a small group Bible study during the sharing time a young couple was worried they were on the way to ruin because they had had a fight that lasted for 30 minutes. They had been married only three years, but it was the worst time they had ever had and the wife was clearly disturbed by it. Other couples in the group laughed out loud and volunteered that they had arguments that went on for an hour or perhaps even two. I had permission from Gay to share this, so I suggested that they were all amateurs because Gay and I recently fought for an entire 8-hour day. The group was so disappointed that the leaders still fought. But this is the power of the lust and greed that can happen when you are fighting about money and sex.

Gay and I had been married for 20 years at the time of the infamous day and we had fought about money and sex over and over again. But on this particular Saturday, we both threw off all constraint and really went at it. We were both in disagreement about sex and money but over the years had learned to never talk directly about them. So the argument started over something trivial and escalated into a full-blown war. We both needed to win so neither was willing to talk, only argue. We started bickering right after breakfast, escalated to yelling as we ran some errands, took a lunch break and continued until dinner. We never came to blows but we continued to try to hurt one another with our words until my wife said something so simple and yet amazing.

It was right after dinner, Gay said: "So what you are saying is you want more sex?" My mind finally opens up and all I could say was "Yes" and "Thank You."

Gay said "Baby, I love you and want you to be happy. Please let me know when you have such a strong need. I can take care of that." Again, my mind raced, my body relaxed, and I was so in love with her because she understood me, and I thanked her again.

We were aware of 1 Corinthians 7:4-6 but we were not sure how to apply that to our lives. I was afraid to be naked and unashamed and ask for sex and she was not sure when and how to offer it.

Once I recovered the sense of what had just happened God provided a revelation to me as well and I said to her "So what you are saying is you want me to show respect for you by including you in what I am thinking?" She said, "Yes, that is it exactly."

My actions had always said to her that I did not think she was smart enough to understand. I told her "I didn't think you were interested." But she was, and it was wonderful to have someone to share with.

Again, we were both aware of Genesis 2:18 but I was too much of a man to ask for help and she had been taught by the world that she should not intrude.

The entire day had been wasted. Our passions, greed and high emotions had prevented either of us from hearing these simple ideas from the other. We learned that day that in matters of sex and money the solution is really quite simple. Each of you owns all of it.

So the simple solution to problems with money and sex is this: Talk about it openly, be naked and unashamed with one another. When you come to agreement, write it in your Book of Agreement and Remembrance.

Selfishness in marriage

> When tempted, no one should say, "God is tempting me." For God cannot be tempted by evil, nor does he tempt anyone; but each person is tempted when they are dragged away by their own evil desire and enticed. Then, after desire has conceived, it gives birth to sin; and sin, when it is full-grown, gives birth to death. (James 1:13-15)

The top 5 reasons for divorce

We often get to teach seminars on marriage. At one seminar, I promised to give the keys to the kingdom to the couples when they returned from the lunch break. I would give them the top five and only reasons that couples divorce. If they could avoid these five they would never be divorced.

They returned from lunch and with much fanfare, and I began the list. The group was poised to write down these words of wisdom and to make them a part of their own happily ever after story. Like some late-night talk show host, I announced "Number five, Selfishness". You could see the heads nod and the pens writing it down. I talked for a moment about how they needed to be less selfish and again you could see the body language in the room agreeing that is something they could perhaps learn to do.

"Number four, selfishness." The shoulders dropped, and the sighs were almost audible, but the disappointment was clear. You can imagine their disappointment when I announced, "Number Three, Selfishness" and then "Number two, selfishness". As a matter of fact, the whole room shouted out loud in unison with me when I announced, "Number one… SELFISHNESS".

I am convinced that people disagree with one another not because they are disagreeable but rather because they are, as James 4:1 points out, tempted to follow our "own desires" (selfishness). These desires cause us to be dragged away by the enemy into sin which leads to death. Disagreements in marriage lead to strife and all sorts of other sins that lead to death; in a marriage, death is called divorce.

I think that selfishness in marriage comes in five flavors and each taste as nasty to your spouse as the other. If you get nothing else from this book, please take special note of these - if you can truly get them out of your life; you will have cracked the code on marriage and all other successful relationships in heaven and on earth.

Selfishness in money matters.

How often do you hear of a couple that has separate bank accounts? Or have separate bills to pay? When I hear this, I wonder are you married or are you roommates? The prenuptial agreement is another legal tactic to protect something you have from your spouse. This is allowing something material to prevent your marriage from being a one flesh relationship. These actions take the wedding vows down to just wedding words.

The worst and most common selfishness in money, however, is a husband or wife that has the little stash of money the spouse cannot know about. I have talked to a number of husbands that keep a little stash of money away from the wife "Just in case I want something, and she doesn't need to know about it." I cannot understand what level of lies would be needed to keep that a secret.

Selfishness in time.

"I want some time to myself" or "I deserve some time to myself."

These ideas will cause you to keep score to be sure you get as much time for yourself as your partner does for themselves.

I was heading out to go fishing one day. It had been a while since I had gone, and my work had been particularly taxing for the last month. I really needed a time on the water with nothing more important to do than to decide if I would use live or artificial bait. The problem was that this is an activity best done with a fishing buddy. We had just moved and there was no one close enough to come over and go finishing with me. I asked Gay to go.

Gay does not actually fish. She is not really all that fond of riding in my old truck or the fact that I forget to clean it out between trips to fast food places. I like to fish until dark thirty, which means I am loading the boat after the sun has been down a while. She is done with fishing 30 minutes after we get on the water.

But she agreed to go. No questions asked, no complaints voiced. I did not know it at the time, but she had other plans for that afternoon… she canceled them and decided to spend her time with me. She has never asked for repayment of the time. This was an act of selflessness in which she preferred me over herself.

Selfishness in prayer.

Your spouse needs your prayers and God tells us that the only way to fight evil is by prayer and fasting (Mark 9:29).

When Gay is sick in bed she wants nothing more than for me to take a few minutes to put my hand on her and pray for God to heal her. But to be honest, there was a time in my life that I simply was not comfortable doing that. We are taught by our culture that our prayers are a private thing and so we are not required to pray out loud or with other people. Besides couldn't God hear her prayer for healing for herself just as good as mine? WOW, now that is selfish.

Be sure you are ready to share your prayer time with your spouse as well as what you are praying about. Never catch yourself thinking, "Well, that's just not my thing". Always be ready to pray with and for your spouse.

Selfishness with friends and family.

Decide together how holidays will be spent and what traditions will be a part of your new family. We too often get married and then want to carry on with whatever our family did, and we invite our spouse to join in the fun. Be sure that you have preferred your spouse over any family tradition.

Tim and Cherish

This was a young couple who had come to us for premarital counseling. They had been dating for a few years and had become part of each other's families.

During one of the premarital counseling sessions, we talked through this idea of how important it is for them to prefer one another with regard to family and friends. We stressed how preferring one another might cause offense to one or both families. It was obvious that Cherish was becoming agitated at the idea because her posture changed, and she began to blush.

"Is this causing you some problems?" Gay asked Cherish.

"No, I am just imagining what it will be like to have our own celebrations", she replied breathlessly with a far-off look on her face. "You see, today we have to eat seven Thanksgiving dinners." Then she counted them. Both sets of their parents were divorced, so four dinners. Then there were the three surviving grandparent houses. "All of them refuse to budge on the day and will not hear of consolidation. And we have to eat at every stop or we cause an offense." As she counted them off, her posture became as if she had just finished meal number seven.

But then she perked up and exclaimed. "So, you are telling me to prefer my husband and skip a 20,000-calorie day? And that is a good thing?"

"Yep," was all that Gay said.

Be diligent about who you are spending time with and who you are inviting to share in the life you and your spouse have together. Your friends should be your spouse's friends and vice versa.

Selfishness in sex.

Sex is not to be awarded to your spouse when they work really hard or make you happy. It is also not a time for demands to be made. It is as much a spiritual time as a physical time. It can be an opportunity for intimacy. If you want the best sex ever, see it as a time to serve your spouse and a time for them to serve you.

Your relationship with Jesus and your marriage

Your relationship with Jesus is the most important factor that will cause you to be happily married. I know this sounds a little out there and perhaps even like someone telling you to "Just read your Bible and pray every day and everything will be OK." This is not at all what I am saying. I am suggesting that if you are having problems in your marriage, one or both of you are having problems with your personal relationship with Jesus Christ.

It is important to note the word "relationship" in this advice. For example, I know my congressman exists and I hear from him all the time. I know where he lives and what he does for a living. I can recognize him from the pictures he sends to me all the time. He is known to me, but I would not say we know each other. We have a relationship, but I would not call it personal. I do not call him to tell him about my day and I am not sure he would take the call. I have never shared my darkest secrets with my congressman and if I did, I am not sure he would care.

I have a dear friend named Rich. He can cruise past my house and tell if I am home or not. He can tell by which lights are on if I am still up. He might notice a car in the drive that is not mine or a door that looks ajar and call me to let me know about it. He calls just to let me know what he is up to and we often have dinner together. He is one of the few people in the world that is allowed to say to me "Now, Chris, that is not what you really mean. It's just you and me talking, what do you really think." He will on occasion stop by the house, walk right in and fill up his cup with ice and say, "Just needed to refresh my drink, see ya." He is what I call a refrigerator friend because not only does he have permanent permission to look inside, he is welcome to anything in there.

That is a close and personal - Proverbs 18:24 - relationship.

Do you have that kind of relationship with Jesus? Does he have permanent permission to look inside? Is he welcome to anything in there? If you and your wife will develop that level of relationship with Jesus, you will never have marital problems you cannot easily solve.

Coming to An Agreement (Counterfeit Agreement)

There is a great deal of marriage help being taught that describes how to come to an agreement. The objective is to help couples stop fighting with one another and have peace in their relationship. Note this, a lack of fighting is not peace. I do agree that it is a good idea to stop fighting and "work things out", but it is very important to not mistake this for peace that comes from being in agreement. Consider this, if you come to an agreement that does not satisfy both the husband's and the wife's needs, you will get to have that same argument again with the added frustration of having been here before.

Often disagreement is disguised and accepted because we have agreed through compromise or a protracted negotiation. Or we run out of energy and say something like, "This is something I am just not going to worry about." We are taught at a very young age that we need to "just get along" or that we should compromise or worse agree to disagree. These skills and habits may help us get what we want for the near term, such as a car loan or mortgage, but they should never be seen as equal to being in agreement. And when a husband

and his wife rely on compromise or negotiating or agreeing to disagree as a way to settle arguments, the peace will not last long nor will it be satisfying because it does not bring unity.

Meet Isaac and Sara

Isaac is a young upwardly mobile professional… that makes him a YUPPIE. He likes things in order, on-time and well documented. Sara, on the other hand, is more of a free spirit. She lives in the moment and just loves everyone. They fell in love right after Isaac got home from serving in the Iraq war. He was attending college on the GI bill and she was studying liberal arts. They both finished college a few years later and got married. Isaac with a Master's in Business Administration (MBA) and Sara with a degree in English.

Gay and I were representing our ministry at a conference on the family in Nebraska. Isaac and Sara had traveled to the same conference to represent their church. They hoped to pick up materials and ministry ideas to take to their home church. It turns out they had significant troubles of their own and were secretly hoping to find answers to solve the uneasy peace they were living in their own marriage.

They were involved in a number of ministries back home including leading a small group and a marriage ministry. But like too many of us, they would not want their pastor to know what goes on behind the closed doors at their home. They were from the same area of the country as us, so we invited them to have dinner one night before the conference was over to get to know them better.

The food was good, and the service was fine. But Isaac and Sara were obviously wearing masks. Every time we would talk about anything personal they would deflect and talk about their church or some other couple that attended with them or how much they wanted us to meet their pastor.

"So, you have been married 13 years," Gay asked. "Tell me something you have learned about marriage in those years."

"Well, we were studying a book by Dr. James Dobson in one of our small groups" Sara started. "And it was just full of good ideas about how to raise children."

"Yes, I like Dobson too, but tell me something you have gleaned from being married to this guy right here" and Gay patted Isaac on the shoulder.

Sara looked down and Isaac changed the subject. Gay and I later learned that they had both been contemplating divorce for some time. It seemed they rarely fought with one another and had even tried a lot of the ideas for coming to an agreement with one another taught at the many seminars they had attended. The problem was that they had never quite been able to find peace in the relationship through these agreements. They had not learned to walk in agreement. They did not feel like they were one flesh and were not sure they ever would be. This broke out hearts.

We have discovered a number of methods couples use to make agreements with one another. Some are better than others but often the agreement reached does not bring the peace of walking in agreement. We call those methods counterfeits, here are a few of them.

Methods to come to an agreement

So many couples just want the fighting to stop so they go into a defensive mode. If you are being defensive and simply avoiding conflict, it implies there is also an offensive team playing against you. In other words, many methods of coming to AN agreement depend upon there being a winner and a loser.

Be careful, once Satan has divided your house against itself, he wins and all you get is a false peace. The husband and wife may have stopped fighting, at least about the subject of the day, but they are divided, and a house divided cannot stand.

Jesus was accused of being related to Satan rather than his Father in heaven. The people were pointing at the way the demons behaved when he spoke to them and called this evidence of his relationship to Satan. He answered the accusation by addressing the relationship, not the circumstances.

> If a house is divided against itself, that house
> cannot stand. And if Satan opposes himself and
> is divided, he cannot stand; his end has come.
> (Mark 3:25-26)

When a married couple exercises a tactic, which creates an agreement rather than the true peace of walking in agreement they are dividing their house. I have listed some of the folly we have observed down through the years. These are ways of coming to an agreement which actually divides a house rather than builds unity in agreement. The list is not exhaustive but rather a sampling.

Check yourself and your relationship with your spouse. Are you using one or more of these to settle arguments in your marriage? Are you building your relationship on true agreement or simply coming to an agreement?

Expert Opinion

Too often we will see ourselves as experts in an area and so our opinion is the expert opinion. Even more dangerous is when one spouse is seen as the expert on all areas.

I met Gay when she was a freshman and I was a junior in college. Gay and I were married in 1979 and I graduated in May of 1980. By August of 1980, I had my first teaching assignment in Jacksonville, Florida. She quit college to support me in my last year and never returned to school. We often jokingly say that I got my BS at IU and Gay got her MRS.

In the first few years of marriage, I thought I was smarter than Gay because I finished college. Whenever there was a conversation that required a decision, I would be sure she understood my superior position by expressing my expert opinion. She would push back sometimes but never very hard. We still fought as hard and as much as anyone we knew but I won the arguments by making her feel stupid.

In retrospect, this was a real flaw in my character and my ability to be a decent husband. It is never a good idea to come to an agreement by making another person feel less than they are. But in a marriage, this is at best sin and at worst an attitude that leads to divorce. I should have been asking for advice from the perfect helper God had provided (Genesis 2:18-23). Instead, I was dividing my house and causing her to doubt her ability to be that perfect helper God had called her to be.

If you feel like you are the expert and do not need your spouse's advice, consider this:

> Plans fail for lack of counsel, but with many advisers, they succeed. (Proverbs 15:22)

Survival of the Fittest

The tactic here is to come to an agreement by simply outlasting your spouse in an argument. The agreement depends upon one of the combatants being more interested in the "win" than the other. We see this regularly in couples we counsel. They are less interested in reconciliation than being the one who is right. There is great pride in winning the fight, regardless of what is right, moral or useful.

This usually plays out like this: A couple will begin to discuss a matter, they begin to disagree on the matter, then the fight breaks out. Once the fight starts the argument is rarely about what the argument is about. They have taken their eyes off the facts of the matter and started picking at the marriage relationship. They begin to focus on forcing the other person to see things their way and not on walking in agreement and reconciliation. The relationship changes, separate camps on the matter at hand are established. Someone needs to be defeated for the matter to be resolved.

Eventually, one of the combatants is exhausted and gives up and the winner is declared by default. The end to this fight is usually someone saying something like "I just don't care anymore, do what you want." If you have ever been in this situation, you know that neither you nor your spouse walked away happy about the outcome. An unhealthy precedent is established in the relationship and the house is divided.

The Bully

This process of coming to an agreement is where one of you is simply stronger, can yell louder or can otherwise shout down or intimidate the other into finishing an argument.

Charlie was much larger physically than his wife, Harriet. When they would come into disagreement (most people call this a fight), he could intimidate her into an agreement. Charlie would win the fight by bullying his wife. He never actually hit her, but he was not above driving really fast and aggressive if they were in the car or slamming his fist on the table to make a point. Harriet would cry and hang her head and agree to anything so that he would stop scaring her and everyone around them. This sort of behavior is spousal abuse and is definitely disagreement and not agreement.

Please do not be fooled by the example I give above; women can be the bully too. A wife might teach her husband that she is going to nag him later if she loses the fight. Or she may withhold sex from him to manipulate him into going along with her way of thinking. Bullying can manifest in any number of actions. The bottom line is that if you are using some sort of action against your spouse to elevate you over them, you are bullying.

Compromise

"You can't always get want" is a quote from an old Rolling Stones song and often used with its punch line "But if you try sometimes, you get what you need", when people talk about compromise. Compromise is represented as a great peacemaker because both sides stop fighting and get on with life under negotiated terms. The problem is they have not agreed to do anything except stop arguing about it. There may be quiet but there is rarely the real peace that comes from true agreement.

It takes a few things to make a compromise work.

1) All parties in the compromise have to be ready to **settle for less** than they first wanted or needed.
2) Each party will have to evaluate what the other is offering and **judge** its "worth" against what they are willing to give up.
3) Each party is trying to appease the other to what they want. Offering to serve another to get service is dishonest and selfish.
4) Once the compromise is settled each party has to be ready to live by the negotiated terms instead of what they wanted or needed.

Isaac and Sara

Isaac had a wonderful job that could support the family without Sara working. She had a college degree and wanted to contribute so she worked at the local library. But being a free spirit working caused her great deal of stress. Isaac noticed this and suggested that she should take time off and work on the "Great American Novel" she has always wanted to write.

Sara's pride would not let her husband be the only breadwinner. Isaac was happy to have her leave the workforce and never have that stress in her life again. After much negotiation, they came to a compromise. Sara would take one year off and write. Six months later she had purchased a new desk and computer and she had remodeled one of the 4 bedrooms to be her studio. She had not, however, even created a working title for the book she was supposed to be working on.

"So how is the book going?" Isaac asked after dinner one night.

"I don't know why you feel like you need to push me, I am doing the best I can", Sara replied with a little irritation in her voice.

"I will take that to mean, not well. You know you are six months in and we have spent a little more money than we thought we would."

"Well maybe we should call the whole thing off and I should go get a job."

The problem was that the comprise had created **an** agreement not agreement. The agreement created expectations from each party and implied a need to check on the performance of the parties.

Agreement in marriage is a manifestation of the covenant that is marriage. It can never be performance based but must be based on the relationship only. God sent his only begotten son (John 3:16) not because we deserve such a sacrifice, but because he loves us and desires to perpetuate the covenant he established with Abraham (Genesis 15:18). Walking together in agreement requires us to be in covenant not compromise.

Just get along

This is where one or both is being dishonest about what they really want. They do not want to rock the boat so they do not risk being honest about what they really want. Agreements reached this way end up causing deception or resentment or both. But there is rarely any agreement.

This was how Eric and Megan used to settle things. They never wanted to have the conflict so they would put it off. If Eric was planning to stay late in town after work to play music, he would wait until the last minute to tell Megan. She just wants to get along and did not like any confrontation over the phone, so she would just say "OK dear, be safe. I will see you when you get home." Eric was being deceptive and found that it worked out well, so he made it his way of getting along.

Indeed, Megan got fed up with the last-minute calls. She resented the fact that he would choose to stay in town to play instead of coming home to her. "How dare he treat me like a roommate and call at the last minute. I'm going to really let him have it the next time!", would run through her thoughts after she hung up. For years she just got along and never told her Eric how she felt, and the resentment grew.

Finally, she had had enough and blew up at him and told him the house would be empty when he did finally decide to come home. Now Eric resented her because it had always been fine before, she never complained. Why was this time different? He thought they had an agreement that he could stay in town late anytime they did not have plans. She never agreed to that and had wanted and expected him to want to come home to her after work.

Just getting along is at least lazy and perhaps just plain dishonest. A couple that desires intimacy need to be honest with one another. If you are uncomfortable, unhappy or just plain confused, talk about it. This is called being intimate or transparent with one another. God calls this naked and unashamed (Genesis 2:25). Playing the "get along game" is the opposite of that and may stop the fight for a little while but will not build a healthy marriage based on walking in agreement.

Agreeing to Disagree

This is one of those statements that irritates me to the point where I want to slap someone. I mentioned before that most arguments do not involve what the argument is really about. They are more about us wanting to be proven right. "Agreeing to Disagree" means you want to be proven right even if it is only in your own mind. Your selfish desire to be right is so important to you that you resist doing the hard work of being in agreement.

Some friends were over to dinner one night (Jim and April). Gay and I had started remodeling our 120-year-old home and they were about to finish the last room of their home. We were comparing notes on things like contractors to use, tools to buy and paint colors they had tried out that might work in our house. Jim was describing the awful brown the previous owners had used on their spare bath and how it had been hard to cover.

"No honey, remember, it wasn't brown it was more of a greenish tan", April corrected.

This distracted Jim for a moment, but he picked the story up where he left off repeating that the color had been a rather awful dark brown.

April picked up her cell phone and said "Jim, you're not telling it right. Here let me find a picture on my phone of the old color to show you." She was speaking more to Gay than to Jim because she was looking for a referee to decide who was right.

April was hurriedly swiping through pictures on her phone so that she could be sure Jim knew he had made a mistake. But before she produced the evidence, Jim and I finished with the subject and moved on. April set her phone down and said, "Well, I can't find the picture right now so we will have to agree to disagree."

Gay patted my hand and smiled at me as we listened to the clock tick off a few seconds so that April would not be slapped.

When someone has abandoned being in agreement to the point of saying "Well, we will just have to agree to disagree" is the same as saying "I refuse to listen to you because your point of view is worthless", or "I am still right, and you are still wrong, but I am tired of working with you on this matter."

> Do you see someone who thinks himself wise?
> There is more hope for a fool than for him!
> (Proverbs 26:12)

There is no place for agreeing to disagree in a marriage relationship. If this is in your vocabulary, lose it today.

Coming into Agreement

In 20 years of doing marriage coaching, I have never met anyone that wanted to be divorced. I have however met a great number of people that were unhappy and did not want to continue to live that way. The problem isn't that they suddenly hate one another, it is that they have not been able to come into agreement. So often couples come to us for coaching with a list of broken agreements they have made with one another. There is always an even longer list of grievances they have not figured out what to do with. Divorce lawyers call these irreconcilable differences. I would argue that it is not so much that the grievances are unsolvable, or the broken agreements are a surprise, it is that they do not have the right attitude, practice the right behaviors or simply do not have the tools to solve them.

Remember Eric and Megan? It was not that Megan wanted Eric to stop playing the banjo or stop going to jams or even that she did not want to go along. She wanted him to stop disrespecting her when they got there. And she was afraid to have him drive her home when he was drunk. Eric changed his attitude about marriage and learned to show Megan that she was more important than drinking and playing music. He also decided he could be less macho and allow her to drive him home when he should not drive.

Isaac and Sara had the right attitude and knew every tool ever invented, but they were not willing to change their personal behaviors. They worked really hard at their marriage but enjoyed very little success. They believed that if they said the right things and knew the right things their spouse would be impressed and come over to their way of thinking. We find this to be a common mistake among Christians. Their personal behaviors do not match what they think they are learning. (James 2:14-24 & Hebrews 11)

Charlie and Harriet were in a church, had wonderful friends around them but were not happy. They were really trying to work on their marriage, but they wanted to keep trying to do it their way. They had their own way of doing things and often refused to try tools that had worked for others. Perhaps they felt pride in figuring it out on their own. Perhaps they thought they were honoring their parents by doing things the way their parents had taught them. No matter the reason they continued to try to lean on their own understanding (Proverbs 3:5) and remained tied to the failures of their past. (Matthew 18:15)

In the next chapter, I will walk you through creating your Book of Agreement and Remembrance. This chapter will present tools that will be needed to accomplish that work. They are meant to help husbands and wives as individuals as well as the one flesh team. They should help you personally know your own mind as well as your walk in agreement. Putting some of the tools into practice will be harder than others, but don't let that distract you. There is no time like now to develop your knowledge of the Bible for example. Or to become more trustworthy by letting your "yes" become a more solidly "yes." Do what you can today and keep growing.

Know the Bible

The Bible is the first Book of Agreement and Remembrance. God provided his Word to us so that we can know what he intended for our lives and we can walk in agreement with him.

John and Karen

"But the Bible is so big, and I just don't know where to start", complained John.

"But, John remember, all scripture is God-breathed and good for us. Just start reading regularly with Karen and I know God will speak to you in what you do know." I explained.

"Come on, John let's try", suggested Karen.

"Does this mean I have to stop smoking?" he asked. "It seems the preacher is always bringing that up when I tell him I want to know more about God."

John had been misled about what God wanted from him. Does God want him to stop smoking? Probably. Does God want John to stop smoking before he will talk to him through the Bible? Definitely not. His preacher was likely well intended by telling John that his addiction was a stronghold that allowed Satan to have a foothold in his life. But I bet the preacher never intended to have John use that as a reason to not search the scriptures for the truth and direction in his life.

I confessed to John that I was a smoker for the first 10 years of my walk with Christ. Did Christ want me to stop? I think he did. But I am 100% positive that Christ wanted me to understand that and so he did not withhold his teaching from me for those 10 years.

Perhaps Eve did not know the Word of God well enough to put Satan in his place when she decided to first sample the fruit of the tree God had forbidden. Satan's opening question to Eve was "Did God really say?" (Genesis 3:1) I think maybe she had heard the commandment from Adam not from God and perhaps she had never talked to God about it. Your personal knowledge of God's Word is important. The enemy will attack you personally not your preacher, husband or Sunday school teacher. It is you he plans to trick.

Prefer your spouse

There is no one thing that will make marriage easier than when you prefer your spouse. This is principle is often discussed but seldom fully understood. "Of course, I prefer her, I married only her, didn't I?" husbands will often tell me. Yes, but when the time comes for you to side with her for no other reason than you side with her… will you? When there is a choice of where to spend your time, your money, your energy, and attention, will you prefer your spouse?

Last week Gay and I had had a very busy day getting ready for a short trip to a city about 300 miles away. We had gotten up early, packed the car including the 100lb German Shepheard and his things. We dropped the dog off at the doggie resort on the way out of town but had not stopped to eat. We were finally on the way, but we had not eaten yet that day. I was hungry. I asked Gay if she was, and she said yes.

Both of us were silent thinking about where we might like to eat. I was thinking "Man I really do not want to mention breakfast because she will want to stop at the Cracker Barrel." But I want breakfast and I really want to stop at the Waffle House. Both were on the way and right across the street from one another about 20 miles ahead. After a couple of minutes, Gay said, "Why don't we go through Sellersburg and eat at the Waffle House?" I was so impressed it was like she had read my mind. She even followed the surprised look on my face with "Yes, I can read your mind."

I thought to myself "Oh my, I thought that was a myth."

She said out loud "No it's called married for 39 years."

We have had the "Where do you want to eat" conversation so many times in the last 39 years that she already knew what I was thinking by that time of day, by where we were and what I normally like she also knew my preference. She decided to prefer me over her preference. She had suggested what she knew I was thinking for no other reason than to please me. We walked in agreement that morning and I really enjoyed my waffle.

Let your yes be yes and your no be no

> All you need to say is simply 'Yes' or 'No'; anything beyond this comes from the evil one. (Matthew 5:37)

We asked a small group of couples that had been married less than two years to describe the biggest and most frequent issues they have had to deal with so far. One of the wives said, "Trying to pick a restaurant" and everyone else smiled really big, nodded their heads and shouted almost in unison "Yeah!"

"What do you want for dinner?" is asked by husbands and wives every day. The answer is usually "Oh, whatever you want." Then the husband picks a restaurant because he is usually driving, and wife says, "No, I don't want that." Then we start over with the "What do you want" question and the "Oh anything, you pick" answer until somebody says, with more anger than is merited, "I'm not hungry anymore, let's just go home."

It is important to be able to take your spouse's word at face value. This means you trust them. When they tell you something you see it as trustworthy. This sounds silly and simple on the surface, but I bet this is something that has happened to you. The root here is that when you answer "Whatever" and do not mean it, you are either lying or avoiding revealing your real thoughts and feelings.

Too often we say yes to people to make them happy when we would rather have said no. Or worse we say "Yes I will" hoping that a situation will come up that lets us out of the obligation we just made. This is at least dishonest and perhaps just plain lying. Nothing is more detrimental to walking in agreement than when you think you have agreed, and your spouse lets you down. You start to ask yourself "Did we agree or were they lying when we made this decision?"

I was talking with a husband recently and asked him "Do you want your marriage to succeed?"

He said, "Yes, but it takes two doesn't it?" He was telling me "yes" because that is what he knew I wanted to hear. But in his statement, he was leaving an opportunity to blame his wife. I was not asking him about any of the circumstances he and his wife were in, or what his wife wanted; I was trying to understand what he wanted.

Jesus was clear about who we serve with our "yes" and "no" when he instructed us "All you need to say is simply 'yes' or 'no'; anything beyond this comes from the evil one." Everything that husband said after "yes" was from Satan. If you need to add something after your yes, I wonder if you can be trusted, that is, are you trustworthy?

Another good example of needing to be frank and honest is in the way you tell your children yes and no. Do you mean it? If you mean "no" stop there. If something is not part of your life at your house, then say so and be done with it. The worst thing I see parents doing today is counting to three out loud. Does that mean your "no" has a fuse that needs to be lit? Do you count slowly to be sure you do not get there and have to carry out the threat? You are teaching them to not respond immediately – even to God. I find that people like it when I say simply "no" or simply "Yes" and leave it at that. Even children.

Practice transparency (Intimacy)

We like to pronounce Intimacy this way: IN – TO – ME – SEE. Contrary to popular belief intimacy does not mean only sex. Intimacy is so much more than sex. It is what God is talking about when he said Adam and Eve were "naked an unashamed". (Genesis 2:25) Husbands and wives need to be able to talk to one another about anything. They need to be able to share how a situation makes them think and feel. This is especially true if there is an area in which you are not in agreement. Without transparency, you are faced with two choices. One or both of you will be unhappy with the road you are on as a couple or you will need to travel separately. Neither of those is OK.

So how do you practice intimacy? Quite simply, talk to one another. Do it on purpose by turning off the TV for 30 minutes and discuss your day. Perhaps sit down in a quiet place in your home (just the two of you) and ask, "What are you thinking?" or "What do you feel?" Be sure you are not being judgmental with one another when you talk. Instead be thankful your spouse loved you enough to allow you to IN-TO-ME-SEE.

You may be surprised what you learn from your spouse. Gay and I have been married 39 years as of the release of this book and I can honestly say we continue to learn new things about one another. These revelations bless us and improve our intimacy.

Recognize the relationship hierarchy

Simply put the relationship hierarchy is the order in which we are to prefer others. The Bible teaches that we are to "love the Lord God with all of our heart, mind, and soul" (Deuteronomy 6:5). This is our first and most important relationship no others are to come before God. Your relationship with God will lead you to your spouse and once married, God expects you to honor that relationship above all others on earth. (Malachi 2:15-16) Finally, we are to prefer our children and then others.

So, the right order of preference in your relations is God, then your spouse, then the children. There is a strong temptation to elevate the children when they come along and begin to sacrifice the other two relationships. This is especially true in blended families. Children are very needy and do require a great deal of attention, but this attention can never be at the expense of the other two relationships. You do not stop following Christ when you get married and you should not stop being in a part of the three stranded cord when you are blessed with children.

School-sponsored activities and popular customs are great opportunities for getting the hierarchy out of line. This is because they come with an added level of undeserved authority. This leads us to make decisions based on "that is how it is always done" or "everybody at schools is doing it."

Jim and Harriet have three children. Each will go to the same school and perhaps even have the same teachers and will likely be exposed to the same activities as they progress through the system. There is an annual Halloween party at the school where the 8th graders are encouraged to dress in costumes and attend a carnival one evening in their costumes. The oldest child fully participated in the tradition regarding this holiday. By the time child number two was in 8th grade Jim and Harriet had decided Halloween was a pagan holiday that their home would not participate in. So, child number two will have a different experience than child number one.

This was not a decision they made lightly, and they did consider the ramifications for child number two. But ultimately this was a decision they needed to make regarding the spiritual direction for their home and their family. The children would be affected but did not get a vote.

Remember, it is important to never decide in favor of the children that is not first in 100% agreement with your individual walk with God and your spouse. If a decision needs more time to study scriptures, discuss it as a couple or pray about it, the decision can wait. An important part of walking in agreement is being sure you are agreeing within the right relationships and in the right order of preference.

Under what circumstance will you change your mind?

This is the very definition of integrity and trustworthiness. This is where you get to decide who you are personally and if you can be trusted.

One aspect of the story of Lazarus being raised from the grave is Jesus staying on to do the ministry he had promised to do. (John 11:1-7) He heard about his friend being sick, but he stayed in place doing as the father told him to do. He was able to do that because he had the blessed assurance that God was in charge of everything and that whatever was to be was for his good. (Romans 8:28)

Too often we listen that little voice that says, "Maybe just this once." or "Come on, I thought we were friends." We need to be steadfast in our convictions. If you have decided for example that you will not visit a strip club, you need to be OK with your friends going without you. No regrets. The reason you made the decision to never go was to avoid the naked women and all the things that come with that. If your friends are planning a party that includes a stripper, you need to graciously avoid the entire situation.

Some circumstances that might happen:

When is it OK to cheat on your taxes? I know that sometimes I am only a few dollars short of getting a deduction that could put money in my pocket. I will tithe on my return so God will benefit as well, and no one will notice if I change the deduction from the $948.00 I actually paid to $1,010.00 which would qualify me for the tax deduction.

When is it OK to take a few things from work? If they are coming out of scrap but I had better not ask because they might say no - and no one will notice a handful of gloves.

When is it OK to look at a naked woman that is not my wife. It's not like I am going to have sex with her I mean I don't even know where she is… it's just pictures on the internet.

When is it OK to break the law? When everyone else is? Or perhaps when you know you will not get caught.

This is called situational ethics and if you have a different set of rules for one situation than another then you are what Christ calls luke-warm and you make him want to vomit. (Revelation 3:16) It's pretty strong language but the truth. God needs for you to be the same no matter what everyone else is doing. Take time right now and write down your thoughts with regard to the following.

1) I will look at naked women that are not my wife when …

2) I will cheat on my taxes when…
3) I will follow the law when… I will not follow the law when…
4) I will steal when…

Strife break

We were so blessed to have had Herb and Anita as our mentors so many years ago. They taught us this tool from a series called "Married for Life." It is great for breaking down strongholds that stand against unity in your marriage. Here is how it works…

You are having a discussion and it has gone from discussion to fight. Don't try to deny it, you know exactly what that feels like. The disagreement has become personal and you have started to think about yourself. You are not feeling much love for your spouse right then and the only agreement you want to walk in is your spouse admitting they were wrong, and you are right. When that happens, take these steps:

1) Stop right then
2) Hold hands (both hands) and face one another
3) Pray for the situation, inviting Holy Spirit to rule
4) Pick up the discussion in the presence of Holy Spirit… if you need to

More times than not you will realize the discussion was really not important enough to risk hurting one another, but rather about one or both needing to be right. When you decide to seek righteousness rather than rightness, you will find the peace of seeking God is more satisfying than winning the fight you were about to have.

When we were taught this tool, Herb and Anita required that we promise one another that we would allow the other to call a break <u>any time</u>. I mean they made us do the promising in front of them. It was like doing wedding vows, only we were not sure we wanted to give up the right to have a fight. Herb told us to face one another, take both hands and look into each other's eyes then repeat these words:

"Gay, I promise that any time you feel like you are in strife, I will stop what we are doing and pray about the situation with you." It felt so odd but then Anita required that Gay repeat the same promise to me. We could not help but smile a little because we could not imagine a time when we would ever need to do what we were promising to do.

Not two weeks later, Gay and I were in the midst of one of hottest fights two strong-willed people had ever had. Fights like that always escalated to a place where it is no longer about the subject but rather about winning; a situation that can really dig a trench in the marriage relationship. I was at a point where I needed to say something that would really upset Gay to the insane level. This was a tactic I often used to knock her "off her high horse" and put me in a place of power. I had a real zinger all thought up and was about to deliver the knock-out speech that would win the argument. But instead, I decided to show her I was more spiritual than her.

"Gay, remember you promised to stop everything and pray with me if I ever felt in strife," I said as I held out both hands. I really expected to see her head explode rather than actually do it. So, you can see right away my motive may have been a little self-serving. But, she gritted her teeth as I smiled like the smart aleck I was being. She grabbed both my hands with a grip that was meant to hurt, and it did. She then began to pray through her gritted teeth in a voice that was almost a growl. A moment later we were in each other arms, the fight was forgotten. I still do not remember what the fight was about or who won but I do remember that we had invited Holy Spirit into the conversation. The rest of that day was spent in sweet fellowship. Our relationship went to a deeper and more intimate level that day. We were learning how to let Holy Spirit lead us out of strife.

Let me suggest that you pray with your spouse right now. Promise to pray with them anytime they feel strife. No questions asked, just stop and lean on the third and unbreakable strand in your marriage, Holy Spirit.

Rating the importance of the discussion

"Eric, on a scale of 1-10 with 10 being the highest importance, tell me how important it is who you use for retirement services," I asked.

"That's easy, it's a 10 plus," Eric answered.

"How about you Megan?" Gay asked.

"I guess I never think about it much, I think it is important and my nephew just got in the business and he could use new customers" she answers with a shrug. "So maybe a 1, but I really want to help my nephew."

It is obvious this is a matter very important to Eric but only a passing thought with Megan. With this little bit of data, Megan went from wanting to fight her husband to understanding that this was very important to him and so maybe she should hear what he has to say on the matter.

It is OK to stop the discussion you are having on a subject to understand what is important to whom. Gay and I have done this many a time in the midst of "intense fellowship" regarding a matter. We often find that in some cases, neither of us really care all that much about the matter. So why are we spending so much energy and passion for it? Why are we so set on winning the argument? Simply put, we have given into selfishness. We see our need to defend self (our ideas), more than our need to walk in agreement with our spouse.

This rating can also help get your spouse involved in a discussion. I remember Gay telling me once describing of a situation involving her family and the family farm. It seemed a trivial matter to me and I thought she was just relating a story about her brothers and parents. I had listened to the story with what I thought was the appropriate number of nods and uh huhs. In the end, she asked me, "So what should we do about it?" Oops, this was obviously more important to her than me and she wanted to help move it up in my importance scale. So, I asked her "How important is this to you?"

"Chris, this is a 10 and I need you to get involved."

At that point, the situation which I would have previously rated a "2" at most, became something in which I was going to get involved… and now. Not because it changed importance to me but because Gay was important, and I wanted to serve my wife.

Do not hurry

There are countless examples of God calling us to wait for him. If you are ever in a situation that needs an answer RIGHT NOW and you are not allowed to seek God and pray about, it is likely something you should put off or shut off.

The first time I ever interviewed for a management job, I was offered the job, but it was through a recruitment firm. I had asked for some pretty awesome things beyond the wonderful salary they had already offered. I asked for free parking space in a covered garage, an extra week's vacation and a membership to the YMCA. The recruiter got all of these things and called to tell me the good news. I told her "thank you," and that I would need to pray about it with my wife and let God lead us because this was a big decision for my family. Needless to say, she was shocked but asked: "How long will that take?" I told her I did not know because I would wait on God.

Never hurry to make a decision. Instead, seek God for what is the right path. Your prayers will be answered in the right timing. I know from experience that it is easier to be impulsive. As I was telling that recruiter to wait until I heard from God, chills were running down my legs. As soon as the words passed from my mouth I had peace. Gay and I had the sweetest fellowship later that day asking God if this was the right opportunity for us. God answered our prayers that same day.

We did end up taking the job and God poured out blessings on our house that was above and beyond just another job.

Create Your Book of Agreement and Remembrance

> Now the serpent was more crafty than any of the wild animals the LORD God had made. He said to the woman, "Did God really say, 'You must not eat from any tree in the garden?'" (Genesis 3:1)

This book is intended to help married couples walk in agreement. To walk in agreement, we will need to agree on things like our careers and living conditions. We will need to decide if we will have children and if so, how we will raise them. How will we help our aging parents? Will we attend church and what ministries will we support with our money, time and talents? Will we keep to a budget and will we save for retirement? Will we tithe and if so, is that net or gross? The list goes on and on and each decision is an opportunity to agree and to take a step toward agreement with your one flesh partner.

This section provides some ideas which need to be included in your personal Book of Agreement and Remembrance. Whether you are a newly-wed couple or have been married 50 years there is a need to agree. Start with the Core Agreements and then add some of the other basic agreements suggested. Once you have those recorded, start to look around for those areas that need prayer and agreement. Keep your Book of Agreement and Remembrance handy and use it to record new areas of agreement. Finally, use you Book as a tool to tell Satan he is a defeated enemy and a liar.

My first healing

I suffered from extreme back pain as the result of a herniated disc for nearly 10 years. It would get inflamed and I would miss weeks of work at a time because of the pain. I was referred to a neural surgeon who could remove the disc. He said that one day my condition would degenerate and I would come to him in a wheelchair. At that point, he would remove the disc. My pain would ease but never really go away. I would develop arthritis, be a little shorter, and have less flexibility in my back. This sounded awful, so I decided to simply suffer with the pain I had.

One night when I was in pain, I prayed, "Father, I am so tired of this pain, please take it away." God asked me to fast meat… permanently. I agreed with God, I would fast meat. Immediately there was a sound in my back like a loud snapping sound and the pain was instantly and permanently gone. This happened over 20 years ago, and the pain has not returned. I had agreed to be obedient and trust God for my healing. (James 5:15)

Some five weeks after I was healed, I woke up on the middle of the night with some cramps that felt a little like the pressure I used to feel on my sciatic nerve. Satan whispered, "See there that healing stuff if just in your imagination." and "You know you don't deserve it anyway." I opened the flyleaf of my Bible and read out loud what I had written on September 10, 1998: "Satan you are a defeated enemy, I am healed today."

On September 10, 1998, I agreed with God; I am healed. I recorded that agreement by writing it down. The agreement was a culmination of me hearing God's word about healing and then trusting that word. Satan did as he always does. He repeated what I believed and what I had trusted back to me in a twisted manner. There was no need for me to even have a conversation, much less an argument about it. I simply open my Book of Agreement and Remembrance and showed him where I had agreed with God.

A couple walking in agreement is a couple that is truly happy, not just for a moment here and there but for always. When circumstances get difficult, they can still smile and be happy because they have agreed to travel together. You see agreement is more of a state of being than a plan of what and how you will do things. As you build your own Book of Agreement and Remembrance, you will start with the "CORE AGREEMENTS" and build on those as you consider and set vision for every part of your life together. This will put you in a position to be able to say yes to your marriage no matter the circumstances.

Tom and Susan

When we do individual couple coaching we always assign homework. This allows the couple to have some skin in the game and helps them to focus on being a couple that walks in agreement. We had asked Tom and Susan to create their own Book of Agreement and Remembrance.

They showed up on time and we began to review the homework. They had not done very well. They were struggling with where to start.

"We have been doing so well since we started getting help from you guys that we did not want to start a fight," Susan bargained. "And I was sure you are not wanting that either."

Tom chimed in with "Can you give us something you have seen we disagree about, so we can work it out and record it here?"

We realized the problem was that we had not emphasized enough the idea that we were wanting to help them agree with one another and record that. We did not want to create a permanent record of arguments they had and how they solved them.

We had them start with the Core Agreements and creating their vision. They started to work on other areas of their relationship where Satan had a toehold or areas where they were irritated with one another. Situations and circumstances where they could apply what the Bible says and walk in agreement with that. Over the next several months they got through the Core Agreements as well as several areas in which they were not currently walking in agreement. Their Book of Agreement and Remembrance was serving as a great tool for happiness and joy in their relationship. It sometimes took work but the increased intimacy (according to them) was worth every minute they spent.

Our first Book of Agreement and Remembrance

In 2006 I was praying to have more time for ministry. God answered that prayer by letting my corporate job end. I decided to do private consulting to support myself because that would provide the flexibility we needed to answer the call God had on our lives. It wasn't long until we realized that this was an 80% cut in pay. Gay got a little worried one day while she was paying our bills and asked, "At what point do we decide that the business will not support us, and you go get a job?"

"I am not sure," I told her. My answer provided very little of the safety she needed.

We got out our Book of Agreement and Remembrance. We needed to make a decision and write it down. We spent some time in prayer about our real needs and the value of being more available for ministry needs. We discussed how we felt, what we thought and played out the "what ifs." Finally, we came to a decision that matched our vision and could serve as a guide for this season of our life. What we recorded in our Book of Agreement and Remembrance was part scripture (Philippians 4:19 among them), part math formula that considered the business' receivables, our outstanding expenses and our savings. We determined we would walk together in agreement based on this decision.

Some six months later Gay realized our bank account had shrunk a little and Satan suggested to her that we were going broke. She brought that to my attention by saying the dreaded "Honey, we need to talk." When she told me this it was because she was afraid. So, we got out the Broughton household's Book of Agreement and Remembrance. Our discussion immediately turned to sweet agreement as we prayed the scriptures we had recorded and then did the math. Satan is a liar, we were fine, and we continue to walk in that same agreement today.

Please understand, I am calling you to create an actual book. This will be much like a journal written on paper; it's a physical book. It is not some notecard or sticky note that you will put on the fridge with the vacation pictures and your children's school artwork. It is not electronic and stored in the cloud accessible on your tablet or phone. This needs to be something you can take notes in, put dates in, draw pictures in perhaps even sometimes put your name in to prove to Satan you agreed and that he is a liar. Your Book of Agreement and Remembrance must be something that has no other purpose and that you can take in the prayer closet. I have mentioned that ours is a cheap spiral bound theme book that has "Book of Agreement and Remembrance" written in marker on the front of it. It sometimes gets coffee stained and has smudges of PB&J. It is a tool to bring the blessing of agreement and a weapon against the enemy; sometimes life gets messy.

Time to create your Book of Agreement and Remembrance

> Submit yourselves, then, to God. Resist the devil, and he will flee from you. (James 4:7)

It is time to put Satan on notice, he will no longer have a foothold in your marriage. Not only will you begin to resist him, but you will document his defeat in your life and the life of your marriage. Starting here and for the rest of this book and I hope for the rest of your life you will document agreement in your walk with Christ, your marriage and your family in your own Book of Agreement and Remembrance.

Step 1 – Get a book. Remember this is as simple as a spiral-bound notebook, is a physical book and is designated for this purpose only. I am not kidding, stop what you are doing now and go get a book.

Step 2 – In the presence of both you and your spouse, mark the book for this purpose. Right on the cover, call it out for what it is "The Book of Agreement and Remembrance for Chris & Gay" for example. This declaration alone will shake the gates of hell. Resist making this a family event. Remember no one else in the family is a part of your marriage covenant and so will not be a part of your walk in agreement.

Step 3 - Pray over the book right now. Say out loud that today starts a refreshed walk of agreement for (state your names). This is not a time to be shy but rather a time of celebration.

Your enemy is defeated, and you plan to kick him out of your life and document his demise.

That was simple enough, right?

Now move on through these next sections and start recording your agreement. It is possible that as you read these next ideas that others will pop up. Work through them and write them down. An entry in your Book of Agreement and Remembrance should include at least:

The date you put it in the book. It may be that this entry gets revisited over and over, that is OK. Add dates if you do.

A description of what you agreed on. Be very descriptive here. It is OK to record what you were thinking, what you talked about, what drove you to need to decide and who drove the need for the decision.

Scriptures. Always look for scriptures to support what you are putting in your Book of Agreement and Remembrance. As you grow in your relationship with the Bible you may find additional scriptures or perhaps scripture to replace what you had previously used. When you add scripture to your entries in your book, you add strength against your enemy, Satan.

Conditions that might change. It is possible that you know a decision may need to change. Gay and I decided how we would care for our parents when the time came. The problem was that we could not predict what our siblings would be willing, capable or interested in doing. We preemptively decided what we would be willing to do and what we would not be willing to do. What we actually needed to do changed.

One entry – One page. I would suggest that every entry is given at least a full page to allow for additional things to be added. Gay and I once recorded a decision regarding our adult son. As we prayed for him, God revealed additional wisdom through the scriptures. We added the additional scripture to the entry.

Now that you have your personal Book of Agreement and Remembrance ready to go you are ready to tackle creating a vision.

Creating a vision for your marriage

> Where there is no vision, the people perish (Proverb 29:18 King James Version)

Vision is defined as "the act of power of anticipating that which will or may come to pass." A vision is to see vividly in one's mind events to come. The very word "vision" puts us in mind to look to the future and not the past. This may be why it is such a hard concept for so many. We want to rely on what we have seen as opposed to what we believe can be true. Paul calls us to live by faith and not by sight. (2 Corinthians 5:7)

Developing a vision is not easy but it is helpful. Many couples having trouble have either no vision or a very weak one. They struggle with decision making and unfulfilled expectations and they answer a lot of questions with "I don't know." The fact that they don't know where they are going and will not be able to recognize it when they get there, is evidence of lack of vision. The uncertainty makes it impossible for the husband to lead and even more difficult for the wife to know if she wants to follow him. Men like to know where they are going before they start the trip and women want to know what to expect along the way and why they are going there.

Developing a vision is important; it will help you know who you are and where you are planning to go by helping you to react properly to circumstances. A vision will help you to know what is important to you and your family. A vision will act as a guideline but also as a guardrail. If you have a vision you already know the answer to most questions you will encounter in life. Having a vision for your marriage will encourage you to make decisions and will help ensure you feel good about decisions you do make.

As you develop your own Book of Agreement and Remembrance, you should include a written vision for your marriage.

Our experience with vision

As I mentioned before, this book is a collection of lessons and tactics we teach to couples in the context of helping them learn to live happily ever after. Sooner or later we are going to ask them to write a vision. When I assign "Write a Vision" to a couple, it always scares them at first. My advice is to not look for some grand epiphany before you get started. Your vision will more than likely to be a series of epiphanies by which you grow your vision and refine it. Gay and I have personal experience with this in our marriage.

One of my life verses is Philippians 4:19 "And my God will meet all your needs according to the riches of his glory in Christ Jesus." God first showed this verse to me in 1985 when I was convinced that tithing would break me. I knew I needed to trust God more fully and adopted this as part of my vision for my life and for my marriage. It gave me the confidence to tithe because I believed God would be able to supply my needs no matter what I was giving. It helped me believe Malachi 3:10 "Bring the whole tithe into the storehouse, that there may be food in my house." My vision at that time in my life was centered around learning to be obedient.

In 1991 God called Gay and me out of Florida - we were to move to Indiana. The call was clear and in an audible voice. God provided little explanation other than we were to move. I obeyed by quitting my job, selling my house, packing the U-Haul and moving. It took me two months to find a fulltime job. But smaller contract jobs kept presenting themselves that actually paid better than what I was making in Florida. All my bills were paid and my understanding of Philippians 4:19 deepened. I now understood that God had the resources to take care of me, I just needed to obey Malachi 3:10. He was supplying for my needs from his riches, not something I had stored up. My vision now included a better understanding of how my walk and agreement with God had given me access to his storehouse.

In 2001 Gay and I were all set. We thought we had it all. But one day while praying I heard God tell me to read the rest of Malachi 3:10 "Test me in this," says the Lord Almighty, "and see if I will not throw open the floodgates of heaven and pour out so much blessing that there will not be room enough to store it." I had to repent of being only obedient. I was showing up with a little teacup to gather up the blessing God was pouring out. I promised from that day forward to show up with a dump truck and try to haul it home.

That day Philippians 4:19 meant so much more to me. My God will supply but more importantly, his provision is better than mine. When he supplies my needs it brings his glory, his peace, and his prosperity. Today the vision for my family includes tithing as an act of obedience but also bringing an offering of thanksgiving for the privilege of being in his courts and being invited to be an heir of the living God.

Recently we have added Amos 9:13 to the vision for our marriage.

> "The days are coming," declares the Lord, "when the reaper will be overtaken by the plowman and the planter by the one treading grapes. New wine will drip from the mountains and flow from all the hills. (Amos 9:13)

When he calls we can answer because we have come to know that not only will God supply for my needs but also his glory which is bigger than my imagination. With that kind of promise Gay and I have made our vision so clear that fear is now irrelevant in our lives.

Writing your Vision

Having a vision will help you very quickly decide matters before you. The matter will either line up with your vision, cause you to change your vision or the matter may need to be thrown out because it does not align. You will be able to discern if the decision supports your vision, or simply supports what you are feeling at the time.

The first step is to decide to have a vision for your life, for your marriage and for your family. The Bible says where there is no prophetic vision, the people perish. Please understand, if you have to say "I don't know" or "just because" then Satan has you right where he wants you, floating on a sea of uncertainty with no rudder to guide you back to the safety of home.

Writing and then putting your vision into action can be both frightening and difficult. Frightening because you may worry that you got it wrong and will lead your life in a way that does not pan out and look foolish. Difficult because we have trouble letting go of how the world measures our success. Be encouraged developing your vision will reduce fear and build confidence. Vision will first, help you know where you are going. As it develops it will lead you to where you are to be.

Consider an arrow in the hands of an archer. The archer will prepare the arrow for the bow long before he notches it in preparation for shooting. He may trim the feather so that it will fly straight toward any target he chooses. He will be sure the shaft is straight and true. The arrow will be fitted with the right tip for the selected target and slot for the bowstring. The archer will be sure the arrow is the right length for the bow he plans to use. The arrow's tip needs to be sharp enough to pierce the target, so the archer will spend time sharpening it.

Once prepared the arrows will be put in a quiver to wait for the archer to find the target for which he prepared that arrow. Once the target is found the archer takes the arrow from the quiver, notches it on the bow, and begins to add pressure to the string. The archer takes time to be sure the arrow is seated right on the sting and aims the arrow in a way so that it can fly to the target with no obstruction. Once the target is clearly seen, the right amount of pressure applied, the archer aims the arrow carefully and releases it toward its target.

God is constantly grooming us for his purpose. He will help us to be straight arrows in his quiver with finely trimmed feathers and perfectly sharp tips. The best place to start your vision is by asking God who he wants you to be. The good news is that God wrote it down for us in his Word. Start your vision with your favorite scriptures. Don't be shy, you cannot choose a wrong verse in the Bible because "All Scripture is God-breathed and is valuable for teaching the truth, convicting of sin, correcting faults and training in right living." (2 Timothy 3:16)

Take a moment right now and record a few scriptures that point to the life you want. Also write a few of your own words about how you would like to see God bless you, your marriage and your family. This is the beginning of casting a vision. Put this in your Book of Agreement and Remembrance. Leave lots of room for this is entry, it will change and evolve over time.

Core Agreements

Samuel and Ruth

By the time they were sitting on the sofa for our counseling session they already had a court date to stand in front of a judge to be divorced. They had hired and paid for the lawyers, they had separate addresses and had established a visitation schedule for their young children.

But they had been referred to us by their pastor, so they came to see us. I am not sure what they wanted; perhaps for us to agree with the decision they had made. Perhaps they kept the appointment so as not to offend their pastor. Or maybe they wanted to be able to explain to their children, their parents or anyone else that asked, that they had done all they could do.

We talked with them about marriage and how it is God-ordained to be forever relationship. We explained that they could live happily ever after by following God's plan for marriage. I could tell there was something else going on. It was that uneasy look people get when you are telling them something that does not line up with their lifestyle or what they think is the truth. You see it in church all the time when the preacher talks about tithing or is making an invitation to come to lay your sin down at the altar.

We felt that they had already decided to get divorced. So, I stopped and asked, "Is this a one-time visit or are we going to work on your marriage?"

Samuel answered, "I don't know, I will have to pray about it."

Ruth added, "We have an appointment with the judge on Tuesday and the divorce will be final."

I asked, "So are Gay and I just wasting our time here?"

Samuel and Ruth had already decided in favor of divorce and not in favor of their marriage. They had shared their decision with many of their divorced friends and divorced family members. These friends and family had agreed with them that divorce was the right answer.

Because Samuel said, "I don't know, I will have to pray about it."

I shared what God's Word has to say about divorce with him. "Let me suggest you take a look at Malachi 2:16 "I hate divorce," says the Lord, the God of Israel, "because the man who divorces his wife covers his garment with violence.".""

"So, to whom are you planning to pray to for guidance on this matter?" I asked.

Samuel replied, "I don't know".

The problem was, that he claimed to believe the Bible to be true, cover to cover, but, he didn't. This time he wanted to follow the advice of his family and friends and not the truth found in the Bible. He knew the Bible claimed there were consequences of disobeying, but he was willing to risk it this time.

Samuel and Ruth did divorce.

We have stayed in touch with them over the years hoping that one day we will get the chance to see that family mend. It breaks our hearts when we see people base decisions on the lies Satan tells them through trusted friends and family. We know that Satan is the father of lies and desires only death and destruction for us.

Like building a house on a strong foundation there are certain decisions you need to make as a person before any of the rest of your decision will make sense. These core decisions are to be made by individuals then agreed upon by you and your spouse. Please take time to really think through these and pray for peace about them. If you find that you have doubt continue to seek guidance from Holy Spirit regarding them. Once you can make these part of who you are individually then you are ready to make them a part of your marriage relationship.

Your "Book of Agreement and Remembrance" must start with these. If for example, you have not decided to never leave the marriage relationship no matter what, then your spouse will be left wondering where the limit of transparency is. These "Core Agreements" will provide a place to stand when the enemy comes to call (Matt 7:25). You are kidding yourself if you think that Satan will not act like a defeated enemy no matter how many times you put him in his place. So, let's build the base with several Core Agreements.

The inventory

The first three of the Core Agreements are part of something we have used over and over again in the last 20 years as a starting place with couples in marital strife. We know that they can only enjoy peace in their marriage when they have decided as individuals to walk out these three decisions. They are written like three basic questions and I will ask them of the individuals. I want them to start thinking about who they are and what they believe. We call it the inventory and teach it to every couple we work with. We know that if they can answer yes, yes and yes to all three (and mean it) they will be able to learn to live happily ever after. These are so key that I will present the questions in brief and again one at a time to be included in your Book of Agreement and Remembrance.

1) <u>Do you believe the Bible is true, cover to cover</u>? This is important because in any belief system there has to be an ultimate source of THE truth. The Bible is the tiebreaker in any argument, the ideal to which to compare all other things.

2) <u>Is your name in the Lamb's book of life</u>? I am asking if you are saved, born again, blood bought and a disciple of Jesus. It is important that you be able to say yes if you are planning to base your life on Him and His Word.

3) <u>Are you planning to live with your spouse for the rest of your life</u>? This goes to whether or not you agree with God regarding marriage as a covenant. If there are conditions on you agreeing to live with one another then you will be double-minded about your marriage. You will have trouble implementing the principles and tactics in this book.

Keep this brief presentation of these core question handy. If you are ever thinking badly of your spouse or think you are being faced with a problem that has no solution, check to see if you can still say yes to all three.

Now a little more detail on each of these core decisions.

Is the Bible the true cover to cover?

When I graduated high school, I married because I wanted to... and perhaps because it is not what my Dad wanted me to do. I shunned going to college and working toward any kind of career. I rejected the church I had been raised in and took up the life of a hippie. The rule of the day was no rules… just my right to do what I wanted. Problem is I was 17 years old and had no real experience or wisdom.

In the next six years, I did a lot of drug experimentation, drank way too much alcohol, had an STD and, still have a permanent hearing loss from loud rock and roll. In those short six years, I was married, divorced and then remarried. I lived in eight different homes and was homeless for three months. I tried out cults and spiritual journeys from Reverend Moon to Timothy Leary. The whole time I was looking for a way to know the truth and when I wasn't sure, I just made it up. I even once told Gay I already knew everything that was important to know.

Then I developed a relationship with God's Word. I found out how much I did not know and how much I did not understand what I thought I knew. I now accept the Bible as true, cover to cover, and as the only source of truth that never changes and is always right.

Now I am much older. I am a college graduate and have had 4 successful careers. With the experiences God has allowed me to have I am much wiser and by his grace, I survived to acquire those experiences. Perhaps the best and most important lesson I have learned is that I do not have all the answers. I am in constant need of a source of truth, rock solid source on which to base all my decisions. Good news - God wrote down all the answers I will ever need.

Take a moment right now and decide. Is the Bible true cover to cover? Does that mean you will go ahead and have faith in the parts you maybe have not read? This is why it is important to stop and pray about this one; it is a big decision.

If you answer yes then you are saying you believe in tithing (Malachi 3:8-10), that you will forgive always (Matthew 6:12) and that marriage is until death. (Matthew 19:6)

Is your name in the Lamb's Book of Life?

Here is an important little secret about marriage… you can never live happily ever after with your spouse until you are already living happily ever after in a relationship with Christ. Deciding to be with Christ no matter what will cause you to forgive others and to be happy no matter what.

You may not be able to forgive your wife because she hurt you too deeply because she was so close to you. This was the demise of the marriage of Samuel and Ruth. Or perhaps you have been hurt by the church (Christ's bride) and you cannot forgive them. Maybe you even say, "How can God let the church hurt me so?" You may find yourself unemployed or sick or lonely or angry but all of that matters little when you are walking with the prince of peace. When you have decided to follow Jesus, these things matter very little.

I am reminded of a man named Horatio Spafford who wrote a poem that later became the Hymn "It is well with my soul." In the span of a few years, he lost his business in the great Chicago fire, a son to scarlet fever and three daughters in a shipwreck. Yet while on a ship himself on his way to join his grieving wife he wrote:

> Though Satan should buffet, though trials should come,
> Let this blest assurance control,
> That Christ has regarded my helpless estate,
> And hath shed his own blood for my soul.

It is well, (it is well),

With my soul, (with my soul)

It is well, it is well, with my soul.

Being able to say "It is well with my soul" is a key element of living in agreement with your spouse and an important factor in your ability to live happily ever after.

Can you get up every morning and say, "It is well with my soul because Christ loves me, and I love him?" Do you believe that one day the trumpet will sound, Christ will come, and your sin will be no more? Are you in a relationship with Christ that has caused you to abandon the troubles and hurts of this world? Have you received forgiveness and therefore forgive?

Decide - make an agreement with God right now. Write it in your journal and never look back. When Satan presents a new set of troubles (be assured he will), you can let blest assurance control (not your feelings) because you walk with Christ. The trouble of this world matters little because you are His and he is yours. (Song of Solomon 2:16)

You must have an abandoned relationship with Christ. Forsaking all others is important. All relationships in your life are secondary but more importantly, they are subordinate to your relationship with Christ.

I have had lunch with Samuel a number of times since he and Ruth divorced. He has continued to pursue money and women more than anything in his life. He has enjoyed a great deal of success and continues to win awards and promotions for the work he is doing. But when it is just him and me alone at lunch, he hangs his head a lot and says "I don't know" a lot. He is not sure if his name is in the book and it worries him but his need for the pride of life is more immediate and so is more important to him.

Are you planning to live with your spouse for the rest of your life?

Many stand up and take vows when they are married. You said you were ready to have and to hold in sickness and in health for richer or poorer until death separates us. You need to decide if this is true. Every decision you make from this day forward needs to be made in light of the one flesh covenant relationship and not two individuals.

Tom and Susan

Tom and Susan were a couple that had decided to not be married anymore. This may have been the only thing they had agreed upon for years. Their kids were grown so they sold their house and decided to live separately and file for divorce. The problem was that they were both Christians and knew that divorce was not something God would choose for them.

Susan was upset with Tom and Tom was upset with Susan. Neither of them seemed to be ready to move toward agreement on the many problems they had accumulated in their 40 years of marriage. We encouraged them to search the scriptures and to pray together for what God have them do.

One day, months after we had encouraged them to pray and seek, Tom called and said, "we have decided for our marriage."

"What was that?" I asked.

Tom repeated, "Susan and I have decided in favor of our marriage."

He explained to me that they had prayed and searched the scriptures and could find no biblical reason to divorce. They could, however, find many places where God had called marriage a covenant and that two had become one like where Jesus said "So they are no longer two, but one flesh. Therefore, what God has joined together, let no one separate". (Matthew 19:6)

A note about kids: Kids are a product of the marriage not a deciding factor or a bargaining chip when you are negotiating decisions. If your marriage is a covenant your children will benefit. This does not mean that a number of the decisions you make going forward will not dramatically affect them - it just means that they do not have a say in the decision itself… Reference the relationship hierarchy.

The Budget

The budget has gotten a bad rap in our culture. We think of a budget as something to restrict us or embarrass us. We feel restricted when we think the budget will keep us from getting what we want when we want it. Too many of us are embarrassed when we cannot afford something, RIGHT NOW. These are more lies from the Devil. A budget will free you to have what you want and will give you confidence that you can afford them without guilt.

In 1998 I was working really hard and earning more money than I had ever earned in my life. I decided to go fishing one day. I hitched up the boat and headed to the lake. When I arrived at the lake I realized I had not purchased my annual launching permit. And worse, I did not have the $30 I needed to purchase one. Where had all that money gone? How is it possible that I had a great job making great money and did not have $30? Needless to say, I was depressed, and I did not get to go fishing that day.

Soon after that our pastor told Gay that we should "Command our money and make it say what we wanted it to say about what we thought was important." Great words and great advice. The problem was that neither of us knew how to organize our thinking in regard to money, so we struggled for another couple of years. When I say struggled, I mean we struggled with our money and with each other.

Finally, we found a resource that helped us develop and follow a budget. A budget provided a way for us to know how much we were spending and on what. With a budget that we could both understand, we were able to have data-based conversations about money. We could focus more on what we were spending and how it supported our vision and less on worry and hoping that we would have enough money to get through the month.

There are any number of resources out there that will help you with this important matter but here are the ones we personally use and recommend:

Book: <u>The Total Money Make Over</u> by Dave Ramsey – This book was where we started. We read it and took the recommendation literally.

Budget tool: "Every Dollar" <u>www.everydollar.com</u>. This tool is our tool of choice. It has made the monthly budget meetings very short and simple because it allows us to keep up with our money every day.

Tools are an important part of being able to create and maintain a budget. Good tools that are used will reduce and potentially eliminate the stress on a relation caused by money troubles. But for the tools to work and the stress to be alleviated someone needs to be responsible for the tasks. In our house, for example, Gay deals with the transactional items and assigning them to the budget categories. I categorically do not. This reduces the confusion of two cooks in the same kitchen. I can see all the work she is doing, and she works hard to be sure I do. We also are sure to agree on all the transactions at the monthly budget meeting.

Money worries are listed 97% of the time when couples are having trouble; many times this leads to divorce. A budget is an opportunity to agree on money. You get to talk about what is important to you and where you want your money to go. You get to talk about vision and things like saving for college or retirement. With a budget, a couple gets to dream and agree about money. Without a budget, it is anybody's guess how the next conversation will go.

Take a moment to discuss the idea of a budget for your family. Start an entry in your Book of Agreement and Remembrance on this subject. Begin to decide how you will walk in agreement in this area of your marriage relationship.

How to know if you have made a good decision?

You have added a number of things to your Book of Agreement and Remembrance at this point. How do you know if you have added the right things? Are these decisions the ones that will help you walk in agreement? I have suggested three litmus tests to be used to help determine the quality of your decision. To execute these tests will require you to be honest with each other as well as honest with yourself. Every decision should satisfy all three ideas.

Does each decision serve God's kingdom?

Every decision we make should be made to answer the question "How does my decision serve God's Kingdom?"

This is why we were created. Service to God's Kingdom is the first and most important commandment, "Love the Lord with all my heart, all my mind and all of my strength." Any decision made must be made asking "How does this serve God's Kingdom?"

Does it serve your one flesh relationship?

First, let's assume that you have checked your attitude, decided to walk as one flesh and come into agreement with one another and have written about places of agreement in your Book of Agreement and Remembrance. You have both prayed about and feel good about each entry.

Your Book of Agreement and Remembrance is not for and by you as a husband or wife. It is for and by the one flesh, husband AND wife, team. No entry can be a compromise or something that only one of you have agreed is the direction you want to do. Remember to take time to pray together and hear God and then take time to hear one another. There is real wisdom in using the thoughts, prayers, and guidance of the whole team.

Does each decision line up with the Bible?

Let's say you are thinking about a new convertible sports car. You have a good job and the dealership is happy to set you up with a payment that will put you in that car today. But wait, Proverbs says that the borrower is slave to the lender. (Proverbs 22:7) So, is the car freedom or enslavement?

This is something that only you and your spouse work out together. Everyone has his or her own understanding of the Bible as provided by Holy Spirit. God's Word is living and is a lamp unto your feet even as the terrain you walk changes. Your understanding may change as you grow. I encourage you to read the Word daily and share what you are hearing with your spouse. Then allow your understanding to help you with decisions.

Remembering to always walk in Agreement

And this is my prayer: that your love may abound more and more in knowledge and depth of insight, [10] so that you may be able to discern what is best and may be pure and blameless for the day of Christ, [11] filled with the fruit of righteousness that comes through Jesus Christ—to the glory and praise of God. (Philippians 1:9-11)

Sometimes you may question whether or not you are walking in agreement with one another. You are doing the work of entering things into your Book of Agreement and Remembrance but you're just not feeling in agreement. I would ask if you are remembering? Remembering who you are and what you are to be about. Creating a book about agreement in your marriage relationship is wonderful, but how often are you using it to remember your agreement? Just as a Bible on the shelf will never deepen your relationship with God, your Book of Agreement and Remembrance will never improve your marital relationship if you only get it out to settle arguments.

When the Jews crossed over the Jordan into the promised land they were instructed to take 12 stones, one for each tribe, from the middle of the river bed and stack them up on the other side. God had them do this to help them remember the miracle of the Jordan river splitting and letting them walk over on dry land. The stack of stones was not a talisman or made of some magic that caused the miracle but just normal stones from a riverbed. The stones were to remind the Jews and "all the peoples of the Earth" of the powerful hand of God. (Joshua 4)

Your Book of Agreement and Remembrance needs to serve to help you remember the blessing of agreement you have enjoyed. It also serves to remind Satan that you are a one flesh team walking in agreement and that he lost the fight that day.

Some days you may question if you have made the best decisions for your family. If you allow the doubt to creep in, your Book of Agreement and Remembrance can become a chore and not a joy. It can become a tool to create the discord of being in AN agreement rather than agreement.

To prevent these destructive thoughts, it is important to remember why you have a Book of Agreement and Remembrance. It is not a book of solutions to disagreements nor is it a book of agreements. It is rather a way to memorialize that fact that two are walking as one. That as husband and wife you have had the pleasure of knowing one another in true intimacy as God ordained. It is to be used as a tool to proclaim victory over any strife the enemy tries to sow in your relationship. (Numbers 10:9)

I have included a number of tactics here that can be used to defeat the devil when he tries to tell you that you "lost the argument" or that the agreement is too restrictive to your personal rights. We recommend you revisit your agreements and perhaps even adjust them as situations change. But like anything else, these things come about only when you do them on purpose and when you approach them with planning and prayer.

Preemptive decision making

Preemptive is not a word we use very often. The most common use of the word and how I am using it here is to do something to disable an enemy before he has a chance to strike. By creating a Book of Agreement and Remembrance for your marriage you are disabling the enemy before he has a chance to strike and cause strife in your marriage. Here are a couple of my favorite examples from the Bible of Satan being defeated before he has a chance to strike.

Daniel in the lion's den

One of my favorite pictures of a Biblical character is a print titled "Daniel in the Lion's Den" by J.B. Pratt. It is a depiction of Daniel after he had been thrown into a den of hungry lions. He is calmly facing God rather than the lions. He is confident that he has obeyed God so he has decided to turn to God no matter what terrible circumstances he was in.

At that point in history, the lion's den was a famous and very effective form of execution; no one survived it. Daniel's relationship and his walk in agreement with God were enough to stop the hungry lions. But the enemy's intent was to strike

Daniel with enough fear to have him abandon his relationship with God. Daniel's remembrance of his walk in agreement stopped his fear of the lions. The enemy had a plan to destroy Daniel, but Daniel had made a preemptive decision to follow God; no circumstance could change that.

David and Goliath

David was a little boy when he defeated Goliath. We all marvel at this and like to talk about the five smooth stones or the sling he used. But, I suggest that it was his life of agreement with God and his remembrance of that walk that caused David to abandon fear and face the giant.

The story goes that David tells Saul about how God has always been faithful and enabled him to defeat his enemies and says, "He will deliver me out of the hand of this Philistine." This was not wishful thinking on David's part. He had preemptively decided he would be delivered (as he had been many times before) and brought it to remembrance as he told the king about it.

The near drowning of the twelve

In Luke Chapter 8 Jesus says to his twelve disciples, "Let's go to the other side". Shortly after they shoved off, a storm blew up that nearly swamped the boat. The twelve were sure they were about to drown. They cried out to Jesus who was asleep in the boat. Jesus woke up, calmed the water and the storm then asked them "Where is your faith?" (Luke 8:25)

A decision had been made that their next stop was "on the other side." Not just any old decision but one that had been suggested by God himself. They embarked on the journey just as God had instructed. And as usual, the enemy shows up and casts confusion with a terrible change of circumstance. A circumstance that seemed too real and too powerful, so they feared for their life. They began to question where they were. How had they gotten into so much trouble? Why were they headed to the other side? They prayed, and God showed up to remind them that they had decided to follow Jesus where ever he called them.

Each of these stories is about preemptive decision making. Each of the characters made decisions by which they will live their lives. These decisions were made and became part of who these characters are.

We each also have certain decisions we must make with regard to who we are and where we are going. When you are married it is important that these decisions are made together so that you can walk in agreement with one another. These will help shape who we are and therefore how we react to changing circumstances.

Examples of preemptive decisions

Gay and I have decided that I will not be alone in a car or the house with another woman nor will she be alone with another man. Our friends know about this decision and respect it. I remember a time when I was out of town and I needed my best friend to come over the house to stop a water leak for Gay. He had to wait for his wife to be available to come along because he respected our decision to avoid even the opportunity for a rumor of inappropriate behavior.

We decided a long time ago that we would not have alcohol in our house. That decision makes it easy for us to never have a situation where a friend has too much to drink at our house and causes embarrassment.

Children that cannot swim are not allowed in our backyard without a life vest of some sort when the pool is open. We will never have to worry about finding a child drowned accidentally.

Gay and I have decided that we will always forgive one another, no matter the circumstance. That way when something unthinkable happens we already know how we will respond. Because I know my wife will forgive me, it is easier for me to allow her to IN-TO-ME-SEE. By deciding to always forgive period; the sometimes terrible letdowns that come from being in a relationship with another person become easier to live with.

Decide now that you will never leave your marriage. Or decide what will cause you to leave. That way when Satan spins up a difficult situation, you will already have a plan of attack that will disable to the enemy. Take a moment and write those down in your Book of Agreement and Remembrance.

Managing change

Keeping your Book of Agreement and Remembrance up to date can only be done with diligence. When Amos famously said, "Can two travel together except they agree?", he was indeed asking a question. This is not a one-time question but rather one that needs to be maintained and reviewed. Couples that agree and then continue to do the hard work of agreeing as the world changes around them live happily ever after.

Tom and Grace come over in a real huff. We could tell that they were really hurting. Something had changed since the last time we have gotten together with them. They were not mad at one another, but they were not happy either.

Grace's widowed mother had become very ill and could no longer live on her own. Neither Tom nor Grace wanted to move her to a nursing home. So, they packed up Mom and moved her into their home. That's when the trouble started. They had not talked about it or made any decision about how this radical change would affect their lives. They had been empty nesters for some time and were used to doing as they pleased day to day. Suddenly there was another person in their home that needed more care than any of the children ever needed. That person was an adult with habits and customs that did not match the home they had established for themselves. They had made the decision to move Grace's mother into their home without consideration for any of this.

"Grace isn't your mother a smoker?" I asked. "And I think you do not allow smoking at your house." "Yes, that will be a problem," she responded. And Tom nodded his head.

"I have three sisters, I am sure they will help out some," Grace commented. Gay asked, "have you asked them yet?"

Tom boomed in with "It seems Mom thinks we should all always eat together. On her diet and her timetable." This really upset the rhythm of the house because Tom rarely ate dinner at home.

She was hard of hearing and would play the TV loud enough for the neighbors to hear, which upset the peace and quiet they had come to enjoy. But the worst truth for which they had not planned for was the fact that there would come a time when Mom would have to be moved to a facility with 24-hour care.

Their life had suddenly changed, and they have some work to do if they were going to be able to continue to walk in agreement with one another. Grace's mom had been with them for only three weeks now and nerves were getting frayed. We encouraged them to revisit the decisions on their Book of Agreement and Remembrance. The circumstances of their lives had changed. Would some entries need to be updated? Perhaps. Would some need to be remembered and reinforced? Likely.

Your diligence may be different than other couples, but it is important that you do it on purpose. I suggest that perhaps monthly you talk about your vision. Use that time to revisit past decisions or make new ones that will support your vision. That meeting may be over dinner or it might be on a Saturday morning before the kids get up. But it is important to have that conversation regularly and with the expressed purpose of talking about how you continue to walk in agreement.

The budget meeting

Of the problems cited for marital strife and the reason for divorce, Money is regularly cited. This is rivaled only by sex which is cited as a problem at about the same rate. According to 2009 study by Jeffrey Dew at the Utah State University, one of the best indicators of marital discord is what he terms "financial disagreements." Couples who "disagree about finances once a week" are over 30 percent more likely to get divorced than couples that report "disagreeing about finances a few times a month." Disagreeing about finance means fighting about money.[3]

Couples will try any number of things to solve the money problem and stop the strife before they establish a budget.

If you are keeping a budget, good. But are you keeping it up? A budget is only as good as the level to which you and your spouse agree to it. We have had countless couples come to us with the common complaint about money. We help them set up a workable budget and a system to maintain it, but 3 months later they are fighting about money again. The problem 100% of the time is they are not having a regular budget meeting and coming into agreement on the budget.

When I introduced the idea of budget earlier, I mentioned a couple of tools Gay and I use to create and track our budget. These tools are also very important to the budget meeting, but they must also be maintained between the meetings. This means you must assign responsibilities to each of you and agree on how that can be discussed at the meeting.

---

[3] US Divorce Rates and Statistic – Daily Spotlight from divorce.com
https://www.divorcesource.com/ds/main/u-s-divorce-rates-and-statistics-1037.shtml

Before I scare you off from this, our budget meetings usually last about 15 minutes once a month. We have a plan and a vision; the meeting is more to be sure we are still in agreement. Satan has been completely disabled in this area of our marriage and the budget meeting is a celebration of how God has blessed us with peace.

Final advice and encouragement

It is my prayer that creating your own Book of Agreement and Remembrance has been enjoyable and profitable for you and your spouse. I know that God will bless you as you continue to walk in agreement with one another as a one flesh team.

Where can I gather advice and support?

My knee-jerk reaction would be to tell you to read your Bible and pray every day and you will have all that you need. While there is truth to that statement, telling you to swallow the whole Bible which is actually a compilation of 66 books would not be much help. You need solid answers to real questions you may facing right now. Some or all of the following may be helpful.

Be a part of a Bible-believing church

It is important that you are a part of a church (Hebrews 10:24-25). If you are not, start visiting churches until you find one that you like. If you are a part of a church be sure you are attending with your whole family. If your church believes in the Bible, then the teachings you hear and the fellowship you share will build you up and not tear you down. At the end of a service, you will feel like you know Jesus better. You will grow in your understanding of the Bible and in God's direction for your life.

Establish a personal time of prayer and Bible reading

There is no time in my day that is more important than the time I spend with God in the morning. I recognize this as necessary to my well-being, not something I do to check off the list. If you are planning to succeed as a one flesh couple walking in agreement, this time will be important to you both.

It is my opinion and belief that this time needs to be first thing in the morning (Matthew 6:33) before all the other cares of the world come pressing in. This time needs to be personal, not via social media or grace around the table at breakfast. (Psalm 5:3) It needs to be a time when you have set everything aside and can pay attention to God. This is not something you do on the way to work. (Matthew 6:6) If you have trouble praying, it is OK to read your Bible and just listen and expect Holy Spirit to show up to encourage and guide you.

If you will establish this time, I am 100% positive your walk with God will be closer and your marriage will grow in ways you never thought possible.

Other resources

Genesis 2:24 Ministries is ready to help; look for us at www.genesis2-24.net. We are willing, able and ready to help in any way we can.

Your personal Bible is one of the best resources you have. The problem many people run into is a difficulty understanding it and knowing where to start. My recommendation is to try out a number of translations until you find one you are comfortable reading. Once you find that translation, start reading in Genesis and read through Revelation. It may take you a year to read the whole Bible. That is OK, at the end you will have a much greater understanding of what God wants for your life.

Gary Smalley has written an excellent book called Covenant Marriage. This book will help you understand how to be in a covenant relationship and has one of the best explanations on marriage communication I have ever read.

Gary Chapman has written another excellent book called The Five Love Languages. I recommend you read this one with your spouse. In the end, you will have the tools to understand how to say "I love you" to one another. This is very important when you are learning how to walk in agreement.

The blessing of unity

Take a moment and read Psalm 133:

> 1 How good and pleasant it is
>   when God's people live together in unity!

2 It is like precious oil poured on the head,
    running down on the beard,
running down on Aaron's beard,
    down on the collar of his robe.
3 It is as if the dew of Hermon
    were falling on Mount Zion.
For there the Lord bestows his blessing,
    even life forevermore.

Aaron was the chief priest and would enter the Holy of Holies once a year on behalf of his people. Psalm 133 describes him dressed in a robe preparing for service in the temple. He would have to have been bathed a certain way and dressed in a specific robe in accordance with God's direction to Moses. Once he was properly prepared he would be anointed with oil and would enter the innermost room of the temple to represent Israel. In anticipation of overflowing blessing from God for the nation of Israel, the priests would have poured enough oil to flow down over his head and onto his robe.

Mount Hermon reaches 9,200 feet and is always snowcapped. Most of the water in the area is supplied by runoff from the snowcaps of this mountain. The psalmist is telling us that the blessings from living in unity are refreshing, never-ending and constant like the flow of water from a snowcapped mountain. The blessings are stored up just for you and last as long as the mountain stands.

Psalm 133 is a promise for a good and pleasant life living in unity with God's plan. We see abundant blessings anointing us for service to God. A blessing so abundant that it flows down and gets on everything from the tops of our heads, down the face and onto our clothes. Refreshing blessings are like a mountain stream. Finally, God promises us everlasting life when we are in unity with him.

Conclusion on agreement

You are now in a good place to participate in a decision-making process that brings you a life of walking in agreement with your spouse. You have started working on a vision for your family. You are developing agreement in the Core Agreements and you have a good foundation to know if your decisions are rooted in truth and decided in favor of your marriage. You know how to be trustworthy and have a number of tools to use to help accomplish agreement and you know to manage change in your life.

Hopefully, you have begun to carve out places in your calendar to have the monthly budget meeting and your daily prayer time. You have allowed Holy Spirit to have access to your marriage so you can enjoy the strength of the three stranded cord and the blessing of unity. Your enemy Satan has been put on notice and you can show him his failures that are documented in your Book of Agreement and Remembrance.

Mark and Libby

Mark and Libby came over for the last time some 23 weeks after we had seen them for the first time. They came to show us their Book of Agreement and Remembrance. The wanted to talk about how it had worked out for them. Gay got everyone a glass of water or a cup of coffee and we had the usual chit-chat about how things were going, about the kids' baseball teams and movies we had seen lately. It was a different couple than we had first met. They sat really close together on the sofa, they smiled a lot and when one talked, the other listened and agreed.

Mark and Libby have been working through the process of coming into agreement. They know each other to be trustworthy and have recorded all the core agreements in their personal Book of Agreement and Remembrance.

"So, you wanted to talk about agreement," Gay asked.

"Yes!" Libby jumped in, "It is hard to believe how a few simple agreements caused such a difference in the way we talk to one another."

She was excited and went on and on about how approachable her husband had become since they had begun to agree and create their Book of Agreement and Remembrance. She had always been afraid to talk to him because she knew it would become some big thing. It has always been easier to just go do her own thing and let him go his way.

They had brought their book with them and showed us a couple of examples that were easy and some that were hard. I noticed that the hard ones had a lot of things marked out then rewritten. I asked, "What's all this?" pointing at a particularly messy page.

"Oh, well we, ah, disagreed a little right there a couple of times," Mark explained. "What you can't see is the pages we have torn completely out".

It seems that this was a particularly hard decision for them. They had finally agreed but the earlier versions had some compromise and in one case, some bullying. They just tore those pages out, forgave one another and started over.

I was so proud of them. They were on the road to happily ever after and it showed all over their faces.

My prayer for you

Dear Father in Heaven, please let every person reading these pages know you. May they grow in understanding of your Holy Word and in relationship to your son Christ Jesus. Please fill them now and let them know the blessing of walking agreement with their spouse as one flesh.

Amen

Printed in the United States
By Bookmasters